"I'm Home!"

a Dog's Never Ending Love Story

Real Dog Reincarnation Stories.
Plus Animal Communication techniques and excerpts
from Ms. Atwater's Book
Animal Life after Death and Pet Reincarnation:
Answers for all your Hearts Questions.

Brent Atwater

The World's Authority on
Animal Life after Death and Reincarnation

Copyright information © 2000-2013 by B. Brent Atwater

Library of Congress Cataloging-in-Publication Data

Paperback ISBN-13: 978-1463578244
ISBN-10: 1463578245
Hardcover ISBN: 9781439267813
EBook ISBN: 978-1-4524-9429-6
Kindle: ASIN: B003UNK0MC
Audio Book:
R2

Translated into other languages.

3nd printing: 2013 USA
Canada UK, AU, SA check with distributor
Publisher's Price Higher in Other Countries

Visit Brent Atwater's Websites
www.BrentAtwater.com
www.JustPlainLoveBooks.com

This *Just Plain Love*® Book
is given

To: _____

Message: _____

_____

Date: _____

with
LOTS of LOVE and KISSES!!!

From: _____

and

Friend

Acknowledgements

I want to thank each reader for taking time to explore my
Just Plain Love® Books
and for allowing me to share what
I have learned and am learning about pet past lives and
animal reincarnation and animal communication through
my and other individual's experiences.
Special thanks to Michael Wellford and my precious fur,
finned and feathered companions for their contributions
and enduring patience with me and my spiritual path.
and to

Tracy Heinlein owner of Blastoff Border Collies, whose
B24 Sage and FA Blastoff Simmer are the wonderful
parents of Blastoff's My Best Friend.

It is my intent and hopes that this information will
facilitate inspiration, greater perspectives, and expanded
awareness in your life.
I thank those who have supported and encouraged my
journey and the authors, speakers and teachers who
contributed to shaping my consciousness.

My gratitude also goes to:
Special thanks to the NC State Veterinary School ICU
earth angels for watching over Friend,
to Dr. Keith Harrison, Vicki, "Aunt Susan" and Jessica for
taking care of and looking after all my "children."
and to
Each individual who shared their story in this book
so that our readers can derive hope and be inspired by
"all that is."

Dedication

This is written to honor my entire inspiring and beloved
canine, feline, equine and other animal teachers,
guardians and companions with whom I shared my
experiences, learning and life.
From my heart to yours, thank you!

To Thomas Michael Ramseur Wellford,
whose life, love, and passing made my understanding
possible. I shall always hold you and hear you in my
heart, my soul, and my dreams.

To those very special people and fur babies who have
been my joy, and with whom I have shared and share
hope, laughter and LIFE!!!

TABLE OF CONTENTS

Personalized Message & Gift Page — 3
Acknowledgments — 4
Dedication — 5
Table of Contents — 7
Introduction — 9

Reincarnations Stories — 13
Revel Comes Back as Sidewinder — 21
Darby "Walks In" to Riina — 35
Luke Returns in Lloyd — 45
Jody Girl Returns as Union Jack Then Reincarnates
      the Third Time as Little Jack — 53
Pickles Reunites with Joanna — 65
Boco as Baj, Then Reincarnates Again as Rocky — 76
Austin's Carbon Copy — 83
Friend's 5 Reincarnations and Past Lives — 91
    Our Beginning - My Sunday Dog
    Electra 1: Reincarnation 2
    Friend: Reincarnation 3
    Electra 2: Friend "Walks in" for Reincarnation 4
    Friend with a "B" on His Bottom Reincarnation 5

Animal Life After Death and Pet Reincarnation — 135

The Dog with a "B" on His Bottom! — 135
History of Reincarnation — 137
The Reincarnation Premise — 140
Physical Death — 140
The Transition Process — 141
Signs the Transition Process Has Begun — 141
Affirmation to Assist in Transition — 142

Brent Atwater's *Just Plain Love® Books* presents

The Importance of Believing in Reincarnation   145
Grief   145
How to Bring Your Pet's Energy to Earth   147

The Global Pet Loss Hope!™ Initiative   148
What is an Animal Hope Counselor™?   148
What is a Pet Loss Hope™ Ambassador?   149

About the Author   151

The Just Plain Love® Story   153
Other Just Plain Love® Titles   156

INTRODUCTION

If you are reading this introduction you're probably a dog and animal lover or someone you know needs a GREAT BIG HUG!

If you just plain love animals or have experienced the loss of a beloved furry, feathered or finned soul mate, have an interest in dog past lives, pet reincarnation, animal communication or care about another individual who is grieving over the loss of their much loved fur baby, this is THE book you're looking for!

The *"I'm Home!"* book series (Dogs, Cats and Horses) shares heartwarming stories that illustrate the various signs and different events that occurred during the times when friends, family and myself suffered through pet loss, grieving, beginning the new search process and how each of us was led to be reunited with our beloved companions.

PLUS, there's a special section that has questions and answers about the pet reincarnation process and some "How to" techniques to communicate with your pet.

Ms. Atwater offers Friend's past lives and multiple reincarnations as the foundation of "all I know from my heart and soul's experiences during each of my beloved pets' sickness, degenerating health, disease, chronic illness and even sudden or inevitable death to crossing over the Rainbow Bridge.

"I want to thank all God's wonderful creatures who have taught me what I share with you in this book that I write to honor their lives.

Reliving each story inside my heart while checking the formatting, spelling and editing of this book was difficult. I have written this book in a conversational manner. To enhance the emotional connections, I chose not to be limited by strict traditional editing parameters. Since writing is an art, I'm allowed that creative expression."

This book derives its information from research and a multitude of international stories gathered over decades. Each dog's reincarnation is the embodiment of the lessons each guardian learned and how their heart's awareness evolved to a higher consciousness with each death and rebirth.

I hope my research will give comfort, strength to your heart and support what you are going though, plus provide and extend what you are seeking to learn.

It is my intent that this book comforts your heart, reassures your soul's knowing and helps ignite hope, in addition to providing insight that expands your awareness of all things possible and real! I expect these true stories will give you tingles and goose bumps (a friend calls them God bumps) of confirmation and that you can relate to the thoughts, feeling and experiences of each owner and perhaps think

Hummmmmmm,

that relates to what's going on in my life!

If someone has told you "it's just a pet, get over it," I hope each of you experience profound healing from the expanded awareness you have embraced when your beloved animal companions reincarnate to be with you again."

Enjoy!

For future books submit your reincarnation stories to:
Email: Brent@BrentAtwater.com

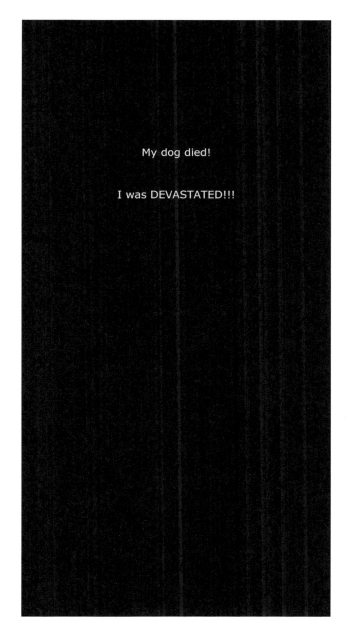

My dog died!

I was DEVASTATED!!!

He was the love of my life!

My heart experienced gut wrenching pain
and
agonizing loneliness.

My life as I knew if for the past 17 years was
obliterated!!!!

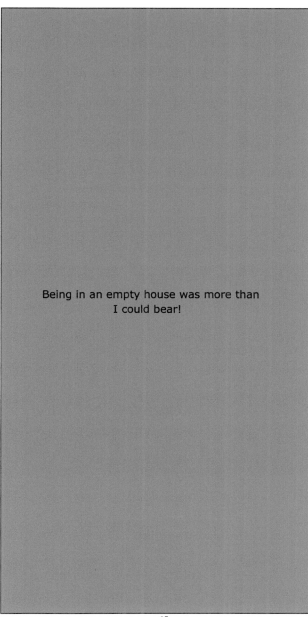

Being in an empty house was more than
I could bear!

For months afterwards before bedtime

I would stand numb at the outside door

like I had done for years at "potty time."

Nights were horrifically quiet!

The emptiness and darkness was
traumatizing

I couldn't bear to put up his photos, food bowls or toys……..
What do I do with his collar and leash?

Today,
when I looked into that puppy's eyes,
there was something <u>very</u> familiar.

Something my heart and soul responded to
and recognized.

Something about that tiny furry fluff felt familiar.

Perhaps it was the way he looked at me,
as if he had done it many times before...

Surely I thought,
not again?!

With all my heart, I prayed for it to be so!

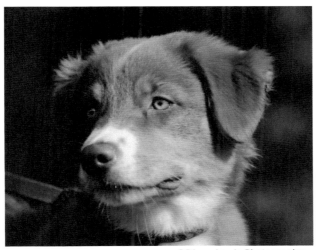
©Diane Lewis Photography

Revel Comes Back as Sidewinder
Kim Young

In 2006 my young Australian shepherd, Revel, died in a tragic accident on our farm. I experienced some of the darkest days I've ever known!

I remember carrying his lifeless body back to my house and crying until I physically couldn't cry anymore. I remember praying and praying to God and begging for a miracle. I pleaded with God to put life back into Revel and offered anything I could think of in return. I felt like if there was a God and He loved me and He loved Revel, God could have given Revels' life back again. I became convinced that all my pleas had fallen on deaf ears.

After he died, the first time I "saw" Revel was that same day. It was a fleeting glimpse that made me think I might be crazy. I had taken his body to the crematorium and staggered out of the building almost blinded by my tears.

As I approached my truck, I saw him sitting in the front seat, beside my other dogs, just like he had so many times before.

His image was there for an instant and then it was gone. I thought my eyes were playing tricks on me. What I didn't understand at that time, was that seeing Revel's image was his way of telling me he was all right.

Leaving the crematorium was one of the hardest things I've ever had to do. Somehow in my mind I wanted to believe it was all a bad dream. If I never went home and never saw that he wasn't there, then I'd wake up and things would be okay.

My husband drove us around for hours because I simply couldn't bear the prospect of going home, opening the door to our home and not seeing him there to greet me as he had so many times before.

One of the greatest lows of my life was opening that door to nothing but darkness and silence. Feeling so hollow and empty, just as I stepped inside, I felt a strange warmth and love wash all over me. I turned to my husband and said, "He's here. I feel him." At that moment, I knew what I felt was pure love and that Revel was around me.

If I had any skepticism in my mind about yesterday's occurrence, the thing that happened next took it all away. From our bedroom, my female Aussie, Chelsea, started barking. It was her play bark, not an alarm bark. I walked in the room to check on her and there she was playing with a toy that was Revel's which I had hidden in my spare bedroom since I couldn't bear to look at them.

Revel normally spread toys all over our house! That toy had been stored out of sight BEFORE I left. Chelsea and my other dogs had been with me. No one had been home, and the door to the spare bedroom was tightly shut. There was NO way it could now be in my bedroom with Chelsea playing with it clearly with another dog.

I didn't see her imaginary friend with my eyes, but clearly Chelsea saw Revel as she bowed and bounced around his toy. When he was alive, this is how they played together. They were best friends. I just knew in my heart that Revel was doing everything within his power to show me he hadn't left me.

I felt a blur of emotions. I was so grateful for his "visit" but I was still devastated. I relived the morning of his death so many times in my mind playing the "what if" game. What if I hadn't gone to the barn that morning? What if any of a million other things had happened that wouldn't have put him in that place in that particular time when he died? I would play it out differently in my mind a thousand times and try to change the outcome. I would relive his last day and beat myself up over and over again for not playing Frisbee with him that afternoon.

It was his favorite game. I had put it off that day thinking we had all the time in the world.

The day before Revel died, my car was stolen. That seemed like a pretty big deal at the time. I'd spent the day dealing with the insurance company and police and hadn't taken time to lay with him. He'd waited patiently all day lying curled up next to my feet at my desk.

When Revel died, I realized how unimportant some "things" are. I'd spent my last day with him worrying about a stupid car because I thought he and I had years together. Ironically,
I got the car back within about 24 hours of his death.
I could have cared less. I would have given that car up a million times to have Revel back.

In the following weeks, during my darkest hours, when grief would overwhelm and paralyze me, strange things would happen in my house. Revel would take his toys out of the spare bedroom numerous times. I would put them up and would come back inside only to find them out again.

The TV would turn itself on during the middle of the night. Pictures of my dogs would fall off of the wall and off of my desk but would never break despite landing on a ceramic tile floor. Doors moved with no one near them to move them. It was never frightening because when those things happened, I felt a wave of love wash over me.

I would "see" him only one more time. One night I was walking in the pasture at dusk and out of the corner of my eye I saw a bouncing red bob tailed dog galloping out of sight. It was my Revel.

Chelsea saw him a lot. There were multiple instances in which she played with a dog that we couldn't physically see yet she saw clearly. One night as I lay in bed, I woke up and felt physical pressure on my feet. Revel always slept on my feet. For that moment I knew he was there.

I started to think I was crazy and had lost it.

People don't talk about this stuff and most people I tried to broach it with were not receptive and put it off to my extreme grief. Fortunately, my husband, previously a skeptic, saw it too, so I knew it was real.   I'm sure my dearest Revel, knowing how skeptical I was, knew he had to go to extra measures to get my attention and to make me believe.

The sadder I was, the more he did to show me he was here and that he hadn't left me.   In hindsight, I also realize he was trying to communicate his plan to me. As more things happened in my house, I became convinced he was trying to tell me something. I so desperately wanted to talk to him and know what he was trying to communicate.

As an extreme skeptic I had scoffed at the idea of animal communicators and pet psychics. To actively seek out an animal communicator was a MAJOR deal for me. Actually communicating with and getting information from a dead pet was something I had never believed in.

I decided to use a well respected West Coast communicator since I lived on the East Coast. This appealed to me because in my mind it was a true test. There was NO way on earth that this person could know anything about me or my dog ahead of time.

I was very guarded in speaking to her and only gave minimal information. She actually only requested descriptive information - basically what my dog physically looked like and his name so she would recognize him when she called him. That was it!

With his name and description she started communication with Revel and I was blown away! She was definitely speaking to my dog and she described the subtle nuances of his behavior that only I would have known. She knew things we had done together that only Revel and I would have known. She described him perfectly even calling him "impetuous" and saying that he couldn't sit still while she was talking to him. That was so Revel! She also knew about what he'd been doing in the house moving things, and she was over 3,000 miles away!

My mind was set at ease. First, it was very clear to me that Revel was fine. Second, she told me he said he was coming back to me because we had a lot of things planned to do together that we hadn't done yet. I was so happy (and yet so confused) that I couldn't believe it.

I asked how I would know him. She said that Revel indicated that I would KNOW when it was him. She also told me that he wouldn't wait long to come back.

I didn't know what to think. This was the best news I'd ever gotten and yet the skeptical side of me didn't want to believe this was possible.

On the other hand, how did someone across the country know the things this woman had known about my dog.

I decided then and there, if there was the slightest possibility that Revel could come back; I would give up my skeptical ways and try to be more open minded.

I was not going to shortchange Revel. He loved me in his life on earth and he loved me from the other side after he died. He was trying so hard to communicate with me that it was time for me to trust what I felt, what I'd seen, what I'd heard **and what I KNEW in my heart!** Revel was coming back to me!

As an aside for those that don't believe in animal communication and pet psychics, I was so stunned by the accuracy in the communication with and from Revel, I later returned to this communicator multiple times to talk to my living dogs. Each time, I was amazed at the accuracy of information provided.

After that communication, I felt magnetized to my computer. I needed to start looking, now! Especially since Revel said I would KNOW when it was him. For the first time since his death, I became convinced by the knowing in my heart that he would be coming back to me as an Aussie. I just felt it!

I looked at other breeds, but they didn't feel right. Every time I took a step in the right direction, my compulsion grew stronger. When I was sure he was coming back as an Aussie, I started looking at Aussie rescue websites. I saw beautiful dogs, but none of them "spoke to me." Their stories were heartwarming, but they weren't Revel. I can't explain it better than that. I just knew.

As I looked at adult dogs, I inherently felt he was coming back to me as a puppy. He was young when he died. He told the communicator we had a lot to do together so I was sure he would be young again. Friends would send me more pictures of litters of puppies than I could look at and I'd submerge myself looking at websites. I would see beautiful litters of pups and wonderful dogs, but I just knew none were him.

"Knowing in my soul" Revel was coming back as an Aussie puppy; I became even more obsessed with looking at rescue and kennel's websites. Sometimes I'd sit up all hours of the night or wake up at night and be drawn to get out of bed and go to the Internet to look at puppies.

I then began a very systematic search. There was a web listing of Aussie kennels alphabetized by states and countries. I started there, working my way through them one by one. At first, I thought maybe he'd come back to me through his first life bloodlines. I looked at those kennels and things just "didn't feel right."

Every time I'd look through a website and get the feeling I wasn't on the right track, it was disheartening. The farther I made it down that list without feeling like I was right was very discouraging. I was exhausting my supply of places to search. I started to worry, what if I was wrong? What if the communicator was wrong? What if he couldn't come back?

Despite doubts, there was something inside of me that was stronger and compelled me to keep looking.
I had to! And I did. I was through over 75% of the list, when I came to this kennel in Texas. I knew the kennel name due to the outstanding reputation of their working dogs.

I looked at their website and came to their stud dog's page which immediately magnetized me. The description of him was my ideal dog, it described my Revel. I knew this dog wasn't Revel, but I knew immediately that Revel would come back to me through him. I just knew.

After that, I didn't look at another website. I knew where he was coming from, I just didn't know when or how.

I contacted the owner to see if she had any current puppies sired by this dog. She didn't but she was expecting 3 litters within a few weeks, one of which would have this dog as its sire. That was the good news. The bad news was that this litter had an over a year old waitlist for his puppies. There were already deposits on the upcoming pups and the owner said there was almost no hope that there would be enough pups for everyone already on the wait list, much less a latecomer like me.

I decided to choose with all my heart to believe in the "miracle" of his return. I just clung to that and asked if I could send in a deposit anyway.

The pups were born in a few weeks. There were only 5 in the litter I was interested in. When they were a few days old, I saw their first photos. I recognized Revel immediately!

Their eyes were closed and they were in a pile, but out of this pile, this little red merle male seemed to be crawling out of the computer screen to get to me.

I knew it was him.

Before I go further, I want to mention a couple of things. After talking to the communicator and starting on the path to find Revel, things stopped being moved in my house. I was still lonely and sad, but the overwhelming grief passed and I started to move forwards while I searched for him. I think he needed me to do that to be able to move forward himself.

Also after he died and I became convinced that he was still around, at times I would talk to him. I would tell him that I knew he was here, that I so missed touching and hugging him "in fur form." Revel took care of that too.

I had done fostering for Aussie rescue. After Revel died, I was asked to foster a delightful female Aussie. For a brief time I thought maybe she was him coming back to me, but my heart's "knowing" quickly realized that wasn't the case. I adored her, but she wasn't my dog.

Revel had sent her to me to fill the void while he was gone. Ironically, she arrived a few days after his death and was adopted a few days before his return. I am sure that was Divine and Revel's intervention.

Although I knew which puppy was Revel, I was still last on the deposit list. How could this possibly work out? There were more great signs. When all 3 litters were born, the breeder told me something occurred that she hadn't seen in all of her years raising puppies; almost all the pups were male. Apparently a lot of folks with deposits wanted females so they were removed from the list.

In many Aussie litters, the merles are first to go. Yet as people with deposits made their selections, that red merle pup wasn't chosen. Surprisingly, one day I received an email saying the red pup was mine if I still wanted him. I asked when I could come get my dog!

At 7 weeks old, we drove days to Texas to get him. I couldn't fathom waiting another week for him to be old enough to fly or much less trusting him to the airlines. I'd lost him once. I wasn't going to lose him again.

People ask if I was worried I'd get there and be disappointed with the pup. I definitely worried about what if I'd been wrong. What if I got there and this pup didn't like me? What if we didn't bond? I had chosen him based purely on this overwhelming feeling that that was my Revel. I had to trust that. So many things had come into play to make that pup mine, that in my heart, I didn't think I could be wrong.

We drove through the night to get to Texas. We had arranged a hotel for the first night there and were due to pick up the pup the first thing the next morning. We ended up arriving early and it was all I could do not to stop by and pick up my puppy a day early. I hardly slept that night.

Early the next day, we drove to the breeder's house. Introductions were made and then she said something like "let me show you your puppy."

She went inside and got him and set him down on the ground. He immediately walked over to me and sat down in front of me and looked up as if to say,

"Where have you been? Let's get on with it...." In that instant, when our eyes met, all doubt was gone. I was looking into my Revel's eyes again.

When the communicator spoke to Revel, I asked if he wanted to be called Revel again. He said together we'd pick a new name. For weeks, I'd written out dozens of possible names and even had my list of names with me.

When I saw my puppy, I knew his name was Sidewinder. That wasn't even a name on my list, but I knew it was the right name. For this reincarnation, my Revel is Sidewinder.

Physically, they don't look the same. They do have eerily similar mannerisms and the same eyes. A dear friend once told me that the "eyes are the window to the soul." That makes sense to me because clearly it's his same soul. His packaging is just a little different this time around.

When Sidewinder came home, the emptiness left the house. I'm no longer sad when I see Revel's pictures. I'm just looking at pictures of his old body. He's here now, in a new one!

One thing that has blown me away is what Sidewinder knew from the get go, as if he was starting off where Revel left off. He entered my house at 7 weeks old with a Frisbee obsession, despite never having seen a Frisbee before. He found his old toys in the spare bedroom and immediately had them back out all over the house.

He lies on the back of the sofa draped like a cat, like Revel did. He sleeps on my feet at night and is always near me, like Revel. He even destroys his stuffed toys in order to pull the squeaker out in the same methodical way as Revel did. Sometimes both my husband and I call him Revel by mistake and Sidey responds just the same.

Other interesting things: Revel was being trained for agility. He hadn't been trialed yet, however impressively he never made the same mistake twice.

From the get go, Sidewinder has displayed that same catlike prowess and brightness. At an agility seminar the instructor commented: "he never makes the same mistake twice." Clearly Sidey was relying on what he'd learned as Revel.

They say little children see auras and energy naturally. My 3 year old niece was looking at my dogs' pictures and told me she liked Sidewinder's picture. At first I was confused because there aren't any pictures of Sidewinder. What she was looking at were old pictures of Revel. She told me with certainty that she was looking at Sidewinder. Since the dogs do not look physically similar, I believe she was seeing the same energy.

That's just one more incident to reinforce what I absolutely believe to be true. My Sidewinder is a reincarnated version of my Revel. Almost every day something shows me my 2 dogs are the same soul. God heard my prayers as I cried over Revel's lifeless body. He brought him back to me. Since then, many things have changed in my life and my mind has been opened to and aware of things I never believed possible.

My world is a much more beautiful place because I know death isn't final, and that the Universe holds endless possibilities when we open our heart and minds to just trust and believe...

©Diane Lewis Photography

Darby "Walks In" to Riina
Ann

On August 27th 2005 at approximately 11:30 pm I held my special sweet heart dog Darby in my arms as the Vet helped her pass on. She was nine years old and I wanted oh so many more years with her. I wrote a poem after I got home from the vets office. I was completely devastated and could not imagine my life without Darby.

In October on a Sunday night, about 2 months after Darby passed; I was searching the internet on pet loss

DARBY
Kurpas' Darby N Red Velvet
July 24, 1996 - August 27, 2005

My Angel Darby

I smell a fragrance from the valley carried in a breeze
The wind softly touches my fur then moves through the trees
My eyes see golden leaves and clouds of winter white
Tiny angels with halos will visit me each night
I stand on a soft cloud a rainbow overhead
An angel with glorious wings is stroking my head
As a delicate wind enshrouds me a soft stroke on my cheek
I've been touched by an angel and now I am at peace
Love has no boundaries
I'll watch over you
I'll wait for you

I held my sweet Darby in my arms telling her how much
I loved her and it was OK for her to go, as the vet
helped her pass to a beautiful place.
A part of me went with her. I miss her so.

sites to help find some solace. I came across a web site that had a page on pet reincarnation I think I read that page at least a dozen times. I had never really thought about the possibility of pets reincarnating but I needed to know more.

First thing Monday morning I called the animal communicator that had this article on her site to set up an appointment with her for a consultation. I had to wait until the following Friday. That was a long week for me. Friday at the appointment time I called her.

When she answered the phone she was laughing and said that Darby is a chatter box and knew the appointment time and had been bugging her.

She began to tell me things she could not possibly have known about Darby since I had not given her any information prior to the appointment. She was right on with so many things she told me. I was so emotional during this call. Close to the end of the session I asked her if Darby planned to return to me.

She said absolutely and that Darby had been with me through many lifetimes. I was so excited and skeptical all at the same time. I had never dreamed this could happen. So I asked her, how does this happen? She said she felt there are a few ways this can happen.

According to that communicator's knowledge: One, you find a litter of puppies you are interested in and in that litter you pick a puppy. Another way is to find an older dog, not old, put older then a puppy. Another way is that a puppy will be born and Darby will guide you to her.

I chose to look for a puppy that had made a "walk in" agreement with Darby. Then I was to contact the animal communicator and she would do a reading with Darby and the puppy. I could not imagine in my mind how this could possibly work.

Darby had some requirements she told the animal communicator. Darby wanted to have a tail, be female again if possible, she did not want to be white and she wanted to be healthy.

When she was a little over a year old Darby had vaccinosis caused by her Rabies vaccine. I'd worked with Darby keeping her as healthy as possible for 8 + years. Her body finally gave up. Being healthy was very important to her.

Personally, I had decided on getting a Finnish Lapphund. I had done a lot of research on the breed and knew this was the breed I wanted. Of course I picked a breed that is quite rare here in the US. I started contacting people in Finland. Now I do not speak Finnish so this was an adventure all by itself.

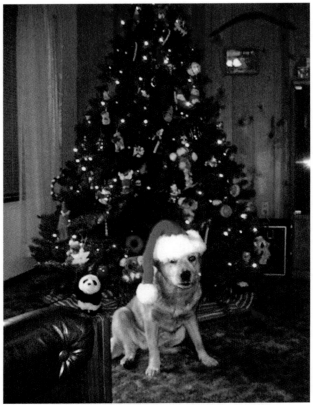

I had located a couple of litters through kennels I thought would be reputable. I had the animal communicator do a reading on a couple of puppies and the answer was they had not made a "walk in" arrangement with Darby.

January of 2006 a litter was born in Denmark that I was very interested in and I contacted the owner who (thank heaven) spoke English. There were 12 pups in the litter, 7 females and 5 males. The owner and I had lots of conversations. She knew what I wanted in structure and temperament and of course a female. Finnish Lapphund temperaments are wonderful.

They are very sweet, kind and affectionate dogs just like my Darby is. Australian Cattle dogs can be a handful in many ways but my Darby was very sweet.

So as the puppies grew the owner sent me pictures every week and I looked at female puppy pictures. The puppy I picked was also the female that the puppy's guardian had picked for me or thought I would like. It was a difficult decision since all the pups were very cute.

Reincarnation is not a subject that many can embrace and I had not yet gone through the process so how could I feel with total assurance it can actually happen.

One day I got brave and told the owner I was hoping this puppy would be my sweet Darby's reincarnated soul. She was so cool and totally believed in reincarnation.

I contacted the animal communicator to do the reading for me to see if this puppy's soul had contracted with Darby to be the new reincarnation body. The answer was yes and the animal communicator said Darby was so excited and loved the little girl we had picked.

I was so very excited and began making arrangements to get the pup to the US. Several things happened that delayed getting her to. She finally arrived in Denver.

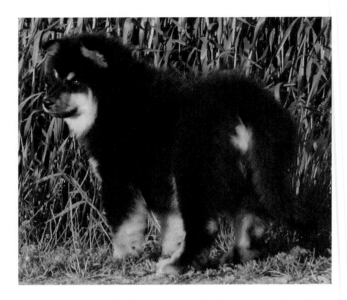

Riina was not feeling too good when we got her. She had a bladder infection and an upper respiratory infection most likely due to the long flight and the climate change.

The first time I saw her I was very emotional and the thoughts of having my sweet Darby back was overwhelming. She was adorable. Knowing that Riina was not feeling very well, I asked the animal communicator to speak with Darby and tell her to wait until I got Riina over her health issues.

I was told there is no time in heaven as it is here so not to worry. It was me that could hardly wait for this transition to begin.

From the beginning Riina's temperament was very aloof with us. Very unlike puppy behavior, especially a Finnish Lapphund puppy.

I watched her like a hawk and anticipated everything she did looking for any passed traits I could recognize of Darby. I kept thinking this is not going to happen because I saw nothing that I could recognize as a Darby trait.

Riina was a puppy that didn't want to play ball, give hugs or kisses, or care if she was with you. She pretty much did her own thing. She was very aloof. I came to realize and understand later there was a reason she was this way.

If you think about it, why would Riina want to become attached to us when our agreement was to move on after Darby's spirit "walked into" her body.

One afternoon I was sitting on the couch and Riina had lain down in the hallway. I could see her from where I was sitting and I called her to me, clapping my hands and encouraging her to come to me. She just looked at me, typical Riina reaction. She didn't move and went off to sleep. In about 5 minutes she woke up and ran to me jumped on my lap, placed her legs around my neck and began kissing my face and pressed her little chest against me. Her tail was wagging like crazy. Talk about heart pounding emotion and the tears were streaming down my face.

I KNEW IN MY HEART THIS WAS DARBY. This was the first sign the transition had begun. The next few months that followed I recognized more and more of Darby.

There were times when I knew it was Riina one minute and Darby the next. I asked the animal communicator why it was taking so long and she said that Darby's spirit was indeed popping in and out of the delivery body.

Since Riina and Darby have very strong personalities sometimes the "walk in" and "soul braiding" process will take more time (some soul transitions happen right away while others can take months), for each of the participating soul's to adjust to their initial agreement.

One afternoon I had Riina outside with me and I threw the ball for her to chase. Now Riina would just look at me as if to say if you want it you go get it. Well this afternoon Riina did the Darby roo roo, fetched the ball and brought it back to me and was ready to go again with another roo roo, which means throw the ball. That was a definite Darby trait she did all the time in her past life.

Other things that Darby used to do was after she had eaten, she would pick up her bowl and bring it to me as if to say (got anymore)? One evening right after feeding, she brought her dish to me. I knew that was Darby. Another trait was when I was sitting she would rest her head on my knee and stare into my eyes with so much love. Rinna soon became so affectionate, happy, content and always at my side. I was thrilled!

"I'm Home!" a Dog's Never Ending Love Story

I am blessed to have Darby show so many traits from her past life to me. In the beginning or when the transition began, it was so obvious to my husband and me when Darby was with us and when Riina was here. Definite things that Darby used to do she was doing them again all on her own.

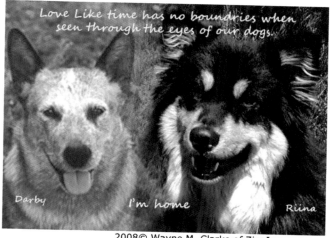

2008© Wayne M. Clarke of ZinaImage.ws

I asked the animal communicator to do another reading because I wanted to know how she was doing and how she felt. These are her words from my sweet Darby. "Feels great inside and out... Very 'spiritual' if that makes sense to you... Loves her new body and said 'we did good'... Not you and I, you and HER... She is very happy. Like from the soul outward.... Like her being is happy""

Riina the delivery soul had moved on and Darby is with me again. She even comes to the name Darby even though I call her Riina Darby Do. I find it very hard to put into words the way I feel. This process is the most amazing thing that has ever happened in my life. It is a true blessing and a wonder to have my sweet Darby back with me again. My Riina Darby Do.

Luke Returns in Lloyd
Suzanne and Jessica Mills from Brisbane,
Queensland, Australia

Luke our black and white border collie was adopted
at 9 months old before Jessica was born. Luke was my
biggest support throughout a 5 year family episode. He
was my 'rock' and without him I would never had

remained strong. Luke held our family together. He was a beautiful example of courage and strength who taught me to stand my ground.

My 11 years old "Luke" passed away in June 2007 after a battle with throat cancer. Luke was a well-mannered dog and many people referred to him as a "gentleman of a dog." Before he died the homeopath who was treating Luke told me that Luke was worried about me as we had not finished our journey together. There were no borders available at the time and I was not ready for him to leave me.

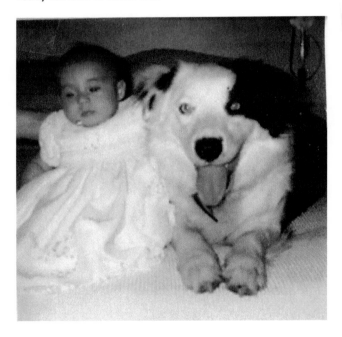

A friend of a friend has a stunning black and white border named "Stormy." She also had recently rehabilitated an old rescue border named "Chloe." We believed that Chloe was pregnant to Stormy (we were not really sure but she was eating heaps).

Five weeks later I was walking my spaniel past our veterinary clinic and the vet called me in to see a litter of lemon and white borders. They were beautiful and the owner asked me to consider adopting the last one. The puppy's owner's name was "Luke" which was quite a coincidence.

My daughter bonded with a lemon pup. He was beautiful but I did not buy him as my gut told me that Stormy was going to bring our Luke back into the world. How was I to decide? If I went with the yet to be born pups, how would I pick?

My daughter Jessica did not mind which pup we had so long as it was our Luke. I was very concerned that I would not see the signs. I chose not to get the lemon pup as there was a University exam that I needed to sit in within two day's time and I was reluctant to leave a six week old pup alone for the whole day since he had just joined our household.

My friends were also trying to discourage me from taking the lemon pup as he was from a strong working line and I wanted a family pet. The exam was cancelled and when I called to reconsider the lemon puppy he was already adopted.

Four weeks later, we found out that Chloe did not end up having puppies at all. The news that Chloe was not pregnant came on Jessica's 12th birthday. I asked Jessica how she felt about the lemon pup that we missed out on and she said that he was not interested in her and that it was her who went after him. Knowing that Chloe and Storm were not going to have pups in the foreseeable future we looked at a reputable and caring pups4sale site.

There were lots of black and white (our favorite) and other Border collie shades. Nothing caught our eye, although we drooled for a while and then decided to wait. The next day I found a litter of tri colors for sale about 200k from here. I emailed the kennel and told Jessica, but she was not at all interested. That night the owner sent a picture of the last little pup available

Jessica was so besotted by him that she was unable to concentrate. We visited him on July 19. His human family was delightful and the pup came immediately to us. He was adorable! He was still with 3 litter mates and his mum & dad but when he met us he stayed close to us. Jess said it was as if he was saying: "Where have you been? What took you so long?"

There were lots of coincidences surrounding this puppy. The son of the human family who bred the pup was also named "Luke" the same as my old BC. Plus, this pup was born on the 20th anniversary of my best friend's death May 26. The family made us a cup of tea and our little pup lay on the couch between us touching both of our thighs while ignoring his other littermates.

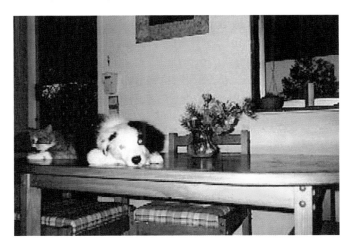

We brought him home that evening and he took himself to the doggy bed in my bedroom and has done so ever since, EXACTLY at 7 pm just as our old Luke would do when he was here. He has never cried or whined like new puppies do. He loves our home and the other pets we have.

Jess and I both had a few tears of joy that this pup is here. Jess tells me that for her it is far greater than normal love and their bond is extraordinary. We tried several different names for this new little man over the first week. For one reason or another they didn't work and just didn't fit or match his personality.

After trying so many different names, we noticed that he always responded better to "L" names. We named him "Lloyd." His soul is familiar to us and he has adopted

all of the good spots that Luke loved. At only 9 weeks of age this little bloke is very mature. He sure is an exceptional little pup and I really don't have to wonder much if the Universe has reunited us.

Luke was a master of 'fetch' and Lloyd at 9 weeks is already showing some talent. There were times when Luke was concentrating he would hold his tail in the most awkward unflattering position and we would laugh at him and call him "Dorkus." Well Lloyd has the same habit! I really am looking forward to the next year to really see what more Lloyd has to show us.

He has even started to sleep on the same pink and beige quilt that Luke did. We're planning on taking him to the beach as soon as he has finished his vaccinations, I can't wait to see if he enjoys it as much as Luke did. Somehow, I know he will!

I now understand that there was no need to panic over these issues. It simply takes the time and trust in the Universe when your dog's spirit is ready to return for you. The time will be right and it will fit. Love will find its way back. It makes me feel so safe about my dad who passed and shared almost the same birthday as Lloyd (2 days earlier) and my mum who died on the day that Luke had his diagnosis. There is much connection.

I wanted to tell you that Lloyd is amazing, handsome, sweet gentleman. He loves to have fun but is happy to veg. He has the same likes and dislikes with food the same as Luke. I am totally in awe of him I feel blessed to be with him. Five month old puppies are generally a handful but Lloyd is PERFECT in every way. Lloyd feels the same way about us and is the great protector.

My cats know him and he knows the house and still owns the car. I am crying tears of joy as I write this as I often do when I hug him. Thank-you for giving me the confidence to choose him. This may sound odd but I often wake at night to simply gloat at this miracle.

"Dorkus" tail

At 54 years of age I am finally learning to trust the Universe. I hope that grieving humans are able to find comfort in knowing that there is more to this

Universe than what we are conditioned to see, and parts that we do not really understand. Your heart will always know and feel what is right!

Jody Girl Returns as Union Jack
Then Reincarnates a 3rd Time as Little Jack
Pete Newell, Sarasota FLA

In the early 1980s, I used to give the stock market report on the radio. One day in October of 1982 when I turned on the dirt road where the radio station was located, this beautiful liver & white female English Springer spaniel puppy came up to my car and I immediately knew there was something special about her.

I mentioned this puppy encounter to my brother and he told me he knew the girl who owned the puppy. She was a vet tech who originally planned to breed this pup but had changed her mind and was looking for a good home for her.

After my brother mentioned that I thought the female Springer pup was special, she decided to give her to me. When I was bringing my new female Springer pup home "The Girl Is Mine" by Paul McCartney and Michael Jackson played on the car radio which brought a smile to my face. I named her Jody Girl after a girl in the bank.

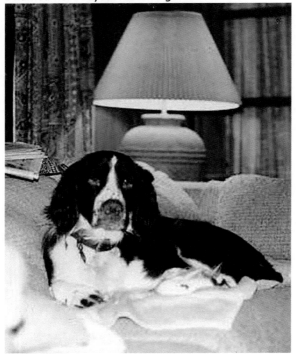

In August of 1994, after giving me 12 wonderful years, my Jody Girl crossed over. I kept hearing "I Will Remember You" by Amy Grant on the radio. Here are some of the lyrics:

"Look in my eyes while you're near
Tell me what's happening here
See that I don't want to say good-bye
Our love is frozen in time
I'll be your champion and you'll be mine
I will remember, I will remember you."

It was my Jody's way of telling me that she didn't want to say good-bye and was coming back to me.

I missed my Jody Girl so much that I meditated and contacted the "other side." I was told "to wait" and the guides would let me know when the time was right for her return. They proceeded to show me a liver & white male Springer Spaniel which surprised me because he was so big and I was looking for a female. They even called him Jack which I thought was too extraordinary. At the time, none of this made any sense to me.

During December of 1994, for three days, I was overwhelmed missing my Jody Girl and was constantly tearing up. On the third day I started to feel better and got back to normal. I wrote everything down in a diary. Looking back, ironically the day the intensity of my pain of losing Jody Girl eased up, was (unbeknownst to me at the time), the day my reincarnate Union Jack had been born - December 19, 1994!

In January of 1995, I had an overwhelming persistent inner urge to look in the classified ads and, sure enough, there was an ad for English Springer spaniel pups. I was thrilled because I didn't know anyone who actually bred quality Springer Spaniels locally. It turned out that I knew Juli the breeder from the early 70s.

1630 OAK Street

SARASOTA HERALD-TRIBUNE / SATURDAY, JANUARY 28, 1995

6870 Dogs

DALMATIAN PUPS -AKC 10wks old, champion bloodline, $300-350 each. All shots. 792-7252

DOBERMAN PUP, full blooded, $100. Call 753-9487

ENGLISH Springer Spaniel Pups. (3) males. Liver & white, AKC, $375 each. Call 953-4304

When I showed up to look at the pups, I picked each one up. One of the male pups wagged his tail when I held him, so I knew it must be Jack.

While sitting around with Juli and her husband, they asked me what I was going to name him. I told them Jack. The husband happened to mention the British Flag was called the Union Jack and suddenly a light bulb went on in my head.

Finally! The name Jack made sense to me. The Union Jack name brought it all together and it right because he was an <u>English </u>Springer Spaniel!

When I got in my car to leave Juli's house after my initial meeting with Union Jack as a pup, the song "After All" came on the radio. It was the Universe's way, I feel, of letting me know Jody Girl had come back to me as Union Jack. Here are some of the lyrics:

"Well, here we are again;
I guess it must be fate.
We've tried it on our own,
But deep inside we've known
We'd be back to set things straight.
It all comes down to me and you.
I guess it's meant to be,
Forever you and me, after all."

Then the first day I brought Union Jack home, he ran up to my Jody Girl's bed and just stood in front of it and stared. A couple months later, I drove by my old house where I had lived with Jody Girl for most of her life and, all of a sudden, Jack got very excited and I thought he was going to jump through the car window.

That's when I was convinced Jody Girl really had come back to me as Union Jack. She recognized her old home!!

Six months before Union Jack's transition, his legs grew so weak I had to carry him up & down the stairs. I knew Jack was getting ready to cross over so I would hug and kiss him when I carried him.

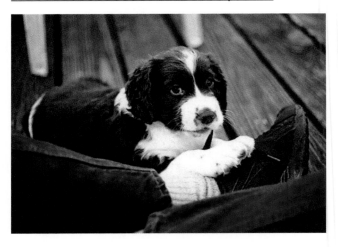

In early February of 2008, my beloved Union Jack, after giving me 13 loving and faithful years, crossed over. I was devastated to put it mildly. I still am! Jack was my faithful and loving companion who blessed my life for 13 years. I was listless and so lost without him.

The other side has always communicated with me by giving me flashes of fluorescent blue at significant times. The "lost in a daydream of blue" lyrics alerted me to the fact that this particular song would have spiritual significance to me.

So when Union Jack crossed over, and before Little Jack was born, the song from a Volvo commercial kept playing in my head. The song was "I Adore You" by Melpo Mene with the lyrics:

"Lost in a daydream of blue
And I feel so free
And then it's like I fall from the sky
Everything that I see is you
And you should know that I'm
Thinking about what you said
When you held my hand
Oh I adore you"

It was also particularly interesting that they gave me this song because during Union Jack's last days while he would be lying on his bed, I would pet him and hold his front paw telling him to be sure and come back to me. Even the part about "When you held my hand" also made sense. It was Union Jack telling me that he adored me and was coming back to me.

At one point, before Little Jack was born and after Union Jack had passed, Union Jack's vibes were so incredibly strong around me that I could feel him. I would even turn around to see if he was there. Of note, Union Jack's vibes stopped being around me when Little Jack was born, although I did not know he had reincarnated at that time.

All during March of 2008, I kept hearing Paul McCartney's song "Simply Having a Wonderful Christmas Time" which I thought was strange for that time of year. Why would I be hearing a Christmas song in March?

Then one morning towards the end of March, I had the urge to send some e-mails to a few Springer Spaniel breeders. I knew I was taking a shot in the dark but I felt compelled to do it anyhow. It was the same urge I had when I was guided to the classified ad for my Union Jack in the years before.

On March 31, I received an email from one of the breeders who said I should contact a local breeder named Jeri who just had a new litter born on March 30th.

It turned out the breeder's kennel name was "Yuletide Springers!" I later learned that my Union Jack's father and grandfather came from Jeri's Yuletide Springer bloodline. It was obvious to me that I was being "guided" and that was "why" I kept hearing McCartney's Christmas song.

When I pulled out Union Jack's Certificate of Pedigree, low and behold, all of his Yuletide Springer's ancestors were listed on it which added further confirmation.

All this was right in front of me and I never knew it until I was guided to this information. All those events really let me know spiritual guidance is real and the process of how your prayers are answered! Another interesting note about this Yuletide litter, there were 4 male pups. Only one of those pups had the same markings as my previous Union Jack and Jody Girl.

The other side had really made it easy for me to be guided to the right pup. Because of my incredible spiritual experiences with Union Jack and Jody Girl, I named my new Springer pup Union Jack II and call him Little Jack.

Because he was too young to come home yet, I would go visit Little Jack at Yuletide Springers. I kept hearing "Only Yesterday" by the Carpenters.

Here are some of the lyrics:
"I have found my home here in your arms
Nowhere else on earth I'd really rather be
Life waits for us
Share it with me
The best is about to be
So much is left for us to see"

All I could think about was when I was carrying Union Jack in my arms and kissing him. I know the lyric "I have found my home here in your arms" had something to do with Union Jack communicating to me about "the best is yet to be" as new Little Jack.

On May 27th, when Little Jack was eight weeks old, I brought him home. He immediately started playing with my other dog and was totally unconcerned about his new surroundings. It was like he had always been here!

For about three days, he did a lot of the same things that Big Jack did right before he passed. I call them carryovers which are really confirmations.

One night approximately six weeks after I brought Little Jack home, he was sleeping on the floor while I was on my computer. I looked down at my new sleeping pup and super imposed over his body was the image of Union Jack sitting up and looking directly at me for a few moments.

I KNEW that my Union Jack was confirming that he had, indeed, come back to me. This was no hallucination! It was the most vivid heartfelt confirmation I've ever experienced. It was as real as my breath. I knew what it was about and was so thankful to know that my Union Jack was back with me!

As you know, the eyes are the window of the soul and sometimes when I glance at Little Jack, it's like Union Jack is looking back at me. I can see it in his eyes. It sends chills down my spine. When people meet Little Jack for the first time, a lot of them remark how much he looks like Union Jack which I think is a subconscious response because, spiritually speaking, he really is my Union Jack.

I wanted to share my story since a lot of people don't understand or know what I have experienced. Juli the breeder told me pets are our guardian Angels. I know that to be true.

I truly believe this loving soul, who came to me as Jody Girl, and then Union Jack and now Little Jack are reincarnations.

All three of them were/are liver and white English Springer Spaniels and a part of my soul.

I call them my Three Angels.

My Three Angels
Jody Girl, Union Jack & Union Jack II

Pickles Reunites with Joanna

J. Hogan, Coon Rapids, MN

My little Miniature Schnauzer Pickles died on Oct 6, 2008. Pickles was not just my pet. She was my companion having come into my life when I first became disabled and was filled with terrible pain, both physically and mentally.

I was so devastated with a terrible depression related to not only the loss of my physical capabilities, but the loss of my profession. Pickles was my "angel" and lifesaver.

In late Sept Pickles collapsed requiring me to take her to the Emergency Vet Services here. She seemed to improve from what appeared to be a "secondary" type of Immune Mediated Hemolytic Anemia and was sent home that same day on medication. Unfortunately, the next day she again collapsed and was again returned to the Emergency Vet.

This time she wasn't improving and on Monday, the next day, was taken to the University of Minnesota Veterinary Hospital. She remained there a week to the day with every attempt made to save her life. That Monday she required <u>another</u> blood transfusion. The decision was made to stop the battle and allow her to cross over. It was the most terrible experience of my life, to hold her and watch her life just pass from her.

About three weeks passed and my grief was still overwhelming. My neighbor was actually concerned about my welfare and had come over with the "want ads" suggesting that I seriously look for another puppy.

Initially, I had no interest in finding another dog, but by afternoon my attitude had changed slightly and I decided to at least look at the ads. I checked the first ad and called the breeder. The voice was so familiar on the other end. Finally, I asked if he was related to the man I had bought Pickles from. Low and behold, it was the same breeder which I thought immediately was an "omen."

I went to look at his two little puppies. My immediate sense was to buy the "salt and pepper" female he had. Then, I started vacillating between the two. My thought was "oh this one looks more like Pickles...this one acts more like Pickles." Back and forth I went for almost two hours with those two puppies.

Suddenly, I realized that all I was doing was attempting to find a replacement for Pickles, or to actually "find her" again. I told the man that I was sorry, but that I guessed that I really wasn't ready for a dog yet. I was still looking for my Pickles.

I came home saddened and very disappointed! My grief intensified again. I told my husband that I was "never going to get another dog, this was just too painful." I had resigned myself to not getting another dog, ever again.

The weekend passed and it was now Monday. I was straightening up in the kitchen, cleaning up all the junk on the kitchen table when I was compelled to pick up those "want ads" again. As I picked it up, I had the strangest sense that I had to look at those listings again. Why? I haven't a clue.

I picked it up and went to the "dogs for sale page." I didn't go to the next listing down from the puppies I had actually gone to see, but went about half way down the page to a "Miniature Schnauzer Puppies for Sale" which was <u>totally</u> unrealistic as they were in Iowa.

This "compulsion" overwhelmed my sense of reality but I had to call the number. A very nice woman answered the phone. It happened to be that she was sitting at work by her computer when we started to talk. She had one female Schnauzer remaining, "Heide." She sent me a few pictures, but those pictures just didn't "trigger" any feeling of attachment at all. I told her that the puppy was cute, but that when I looked at the picture it just "didn't feel right." I told her that I guessed that I "just wasn't ready yet to get another puppy." I told her that I didn't even understand why I had called her.

On a second note, my daughter was going to be having twin girls in December which I shared with this woman and told her that I should probably just focus my attention on my two new little granddaughters when they were born. Even my daughter in her "feelings" of joy felt and just knew that "my Pickles would be coming home." Then Jamie told me that she was also pregnant and going to be having her child in May.

Out of the blue she began telling me that because of her own pregnancy she had also decided to breed her one year old female, Jorja. As soon as she told me this I felt this "sense, feeling" that I just couldn't understand. Then, she told me that Jorja had been bred on October 8th which was just two days after Pickles had passed.

I can't explain it, but I immediately had this "sense."
I told Jodi, "You may think I am totally nuts, but I think
my Pickles is going to come back to me." Jodi really
didn't seem to react negatively to what I had said about
Pickles coming back. I also said to her, "my Pickles had
her right ear standing up. If one of those new puppies
has her ear standing up that will really be the tip off."

Another weird coincidence about this upcoming
second litter was that Pickles had also been born in
December and I got her in February. With Jorja's
pregnancy, her puppies would be born in December and
the puppies would be ready to leave her in February.
Hmmmmm.

Well, on December 11 those puppies were born.
Miracles abounding in this litter! First, a Miniature
Schnauzer will usually only have four, or five puppies.
Jorja had eight. Jamie sent me a picture of the litter
about two days after they were born. I looked at that
picture. There at the bottom of the picture was this tiny,
light colored little bundle. I just knew that was Pickles.

I immediately wrote to Jamie and told her, "I want
that little light puppy at the bottom of the picture." She
immediately wrote back to me. That little light puppy was
the "only" salt and pepper female in the litter. Now, that
wasn't just the only coincidence.

When I got the individual pictures of each puppy there
was my little salt and pepper female "with her left ear
standing straight up.' Now, that may change as the ears
fill in and grow.

I certainly took that as a "sign," a confirmation from
something higher was letting me know that this was
indeed my little Pickle!

Beside the upright ear there were two other
confirmations for me. The puppy also had a dark streak
down her entire back just as my little Pickles had.

Sweetest Baby Pickles

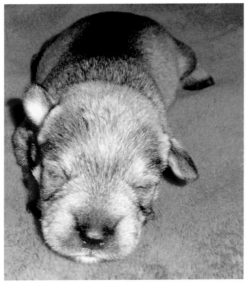

Also a white "heart" encircling her mouth, just the same as my Pickles.   Now, I am just two weeks away from picking up my Pickles.

Three days ago I received another email with individual pictures of the puppies. I started to go thru the row of pictures. With each one I looked at I became a little sadder.

With every puppy, I found myself thinking, "This one is nothing like Pickles. The stature is different. They have coarser fur, etc." I started to think to myself, "Maybe I am crazy, maybe this is all some delusion I have conjured up in my head to appease my own grief.

Finally, I got to the second to the last picture and looked. I became absolutely hysterical. I began sobbing uncontrollably and just screamed out loud, "My God, thank you. This is Pickles." This little puppy was nothing like the rest. She was smaller framed, thinner "fly away" fur just like my little girl. It was as though I had received a picture of Pickles the day after I had gotten her.

I printed that picture out and handed it to my husband as soon as he walked in the door from work. "Ooohhh," he said, "a picture of Pickles when she was a puppy. Where did you come across that?"

He was slightly amazed when I told him that was the "new Pickles." I think that my husband is finally starting to believe in "possibilities." Well, I will be getting my "little girl" in just under two weeks and I am continuing to "believe."

After reading Friend's story, I have a fantasy that my Pickles will be obviously excited to see me too. I have her bed ready, all her toys lined up for her. I am sending a picture of my Pickles along with the new puppy photos. I have always believed in miracles.

When Pickles was ill, I just couldn't believe that God had not answered my pleas to save her. God has never denied my heartfelt prayers and I just "didn't get why she didn't get better when she was so sick."

I 'm glad you had pet reincarnation on your web site. I just knew I wasn't crazy and KNEW I could not be the only person that either felt this way, or had this type of thing happen.

I am hoping that I will have additional confirmations tomorrow when I bring my "new Pickles" home. I did have a chance to talk to her on the phone a few days ago. The breeder Jamie put her up to the phone. I started to call her and say, "Pickles, my little Picky, how's my girl, this is mama..." Jamie said, "Wow, how strange. Pickles immediately started licking the phone like a little crazy girl."

Then, she put her back down on the floor and she immediately started to cry as loudly as if she was "injured." Well, all I could do was cry. I told Jodi, "of course she licked the phone, she knew it was her mama." I think when she gets home tomorrow there will be many "awakenings" occurring.

I choose to believe that God is answering my prayers, I am getting my miracle - it is just not the miracle I prayed for, I'm getting my "Pickles back!

Pickles (II). Today I picked her up. I had to drive a bit, almost two hours. Colleen went with me which would allow me to carry Pickles on the trip back. All the way to Mankato I shared the "peculiar" circumstances involving my coming to find and now picking up Pickles. I assure you Colleen was a "skeptic" and stated so. She did share that she wished she could believe in such "miraculous" occurrences and that if I believed this to be Pickles "reincarnation" she was most happy for me.

Jamie, the breeder pulled right up next to us in the parking lot. Colleen was the first to see little Pickles and all she could say was, "Oh my God, is she cute... she is just something. Joanna you're gonna die when you see her."

It was cold so we got out of my car and went to sit in the back seat of Jami's car. Suddenly there was my little Pickles peeping at us and she was a sight! It was like looking back almost nine years to see my "first" Pickles as a puppy. Jami's mom handed her to me. I had expected her to be somewhat reluctant and fearful of a new person in her life. Not a bit!

She immediately literally starred at my face with a fixed gaze. Then, she just melted in my arms and placed her head on my arm, totally relaxed. She laid there for a couple minutes and then crawled upward laying her head on my shoulder and again immediately relaxed almost going to sleep. She kept turning her head to stare in to my face. I tend to be a somewhat emotional person and the tears just started to flow. I looked at everyone present in the car and just said, "This is Pickles, I just feel it."

Then, thinking out loud I said, "This is the exact position when I lost her, and now it's the way she comes back to me." When I put her to sleep she was laying in my arms with her little head on my shoulder.

I covered her head with her blanket reassuring her that everything would be ok and that I loved her." I nodded to the veterinarian simply saying, "It's OK." She totally went limp in my arms and I knew she was gone.

Now, she was lying on my shoulder, just the same way as when I had lost her. Again, I just could do nothing, but cry and thank God. I can't tell you how many times on the way home Colleen would say, "Joanna, it's like she knows you!"

Pickles slept almost the entire way home except for the several times she tried to jump into the back seat. Of note: my first Pickles "hated" to sit in the front seat and no matter how I would attempt to keep her there, she would always jump into the back seat.

When we arrived home my other neighbor Sue, came over to see our new Pickles. She picked her up and immediately Pickles looked her square in the eye and licked her face. Now, it would seem to me that normally a "new puppy" would have some sort of "stranger anxiety." Never once did I notice any anxiety, or fear with meeting me, Colleen and now Sue. The first thing that came out of Sue's mouth was, "She looks just like Pickles."

I then took Pickles into the house and up the stairs to the living room. She immediately walked down the hall, peeked in at my bedroom, looked back and forth as if to say, "Yup, all the same-still here." She then came back down the hall and sat right at the top of the stairs looking down in just the exact manner that my first Pickles had done for years.

I couldn't wait to show her to my sister Tonie who is nearly 86. I put Pickles on her lap and she immediately faced Toni and started to lick her face as if a joyful reunion. This once rambunctious little puppy was now content to lie on Toni's lap all evening. Not a peep or any anxiety you would expect from an eight week old puppy just separated from the only owners it had known.

Also, Pickles had a small bed in the kitchen where she would always be if I were working there. This Pickles was "immediately" drawn to that bed and lays in it displaying all the "old" positions she would assume in her first life. i.e. "head out the front on the floor," "upside down with her head over the arm," "curled up in a ball on the 'right' side." These little nuances are all too familiar for a "new little puppy" who is supposedly just "learning."

Here's one last little "ditty" about new Pickles. My old Pickles would never eat in the kitchen. She would sit by the kitchen counter and just wait for preparation of supper to be completed.

Suddenly, last week "new" little Pickles started to sit by the counter just below the sink as I was getting supper ready. I was cutting up some food on a plate for my sister. Pickles started barking and jumping uncontrollably. Finally, I took a paper plate and cut a few pieces of roast beef on that plate.

When I set it down in front of her, Pickles immediately picked up that paper plate and took it to the dining room, just in front of the patio doors and then ate. This was the exact "spot" old Pickles would eat her supper. After she finished the meat on the plate, she again picked it up and started carrying around the empty plate just like old Pickles would do too. I just love all of these continuing confirmations that my Pickles is home!

After today, I could never doubt that a miracle has occurred in our lives. God with all his might has given me the gift of uniting me with one of the strongest love's I have ever felt in my life. I feel wonderful, as if this hole in my heart has been healed. I will continue to "update" you of any new happenings in the life of my little Pickles.

Boco Returns as Baj
Then Reincarnates Again as Rocky
Maili

This is a story about a wonderful, beautiful, large and very macho black lab that had charisma like his owner Steve.

Steve was a California fireman, a surfer and known throughout the beach community as social, friendly and gregarious.

Steve had met Boco on the beach boardwalk on earlier occasions while he was being walked by his owner. Boco and Steve shared a mutual admiration for each other   (and there was this pang of "I wish you were mine, and I want you to live with me" kind-of intuitive message going on.)

When Boco was 6 months old, the owner knocked on Steve's door. She asked "will you take my dog? I cannot keep him in my apartment.   You obviously belong to each other." Tears were running down her cheeks, "I can't keep him, my landlord won't let me have him,----- please..... Be good to him, and have a wonderful long life together."

Steve looked into Boco's eyes, and Boco looked into Steve's, and they both knew that they were a team. Happiness and contentment flooded their macho chests.

When Boco was 17, he went out of the gate that surrounded their cottage and was fatally hit by a truck.

When a neighbor told Steve what had happened, he vowed he would never be able to replace such a friend, and he wasn't even going to try. The next morning, without Boco to start his day, Steve was empty. He went through the motions, but there was no joy. Life and his "home" as he knew it was gone. He began to build a new life but there was always something missing.

About 9 mos. later a young woman came to Steve's door, holding a leash with an adorable Rhodesian ridgeback puppy bouncing on the other end. She gave Steve that look that was familiar --, with the words "can you please take my dog? Please take my dog, and give him a good home." Steve named the puppy Baj.

Baj had seen Steve a few times at the boardwalk and would become exuberant wheneve r they would encounter one another.

The young woman felt as if she was "keeping a pre-destined relationship from flowering". She said..."I know he prefers you to me. If I really love him, I have to give him to you."

Steve had vowed that he'd never get attached to another dog again, but some things are "out of our control."

Four years later, I met Steve who became my boyfriend. When it became very clear that Baj was definitely going to be a part of our relationship, I insisted that I meet his dog.

I had them both over for dinner. My children and I instantly became charmed by and enamored with Baj. Even on our first meeting it was so natural to have him around. Baj began to spend nights with us and we would include him in our activities. My children would refer to him as their dog.

When Steve would go on long trips, Baj would stay with us and slept next to me. We had an understanding that we wanted "to keep each other." Finally one day Steve came over and acknowledged the look Baj had in his eyes when Steve said, "okay Baj, let's go home".

Baj looked at me, looked at Steve, looked at my sons and daughter, and walked back towards the bed we had made for him, laid down, and looked at Steve as if to say "can we talk about this tomorrow?"

Steve said, "Well, Baj, I guess you are making it really clear. I think you like it with them better, and I can't say I blame you pal. You have two cats, three kids, all those hugs, walks, you get to sleep in a real human bed every night, take daily rides in the car, beach trips whenever you ask....." With tears in his eyes Steve said, "Maili, he's yours" although in my heart I already knew he was mine. We had connected on a heart and soul level many months before, we just couldn't tell Steve.

Baj got sick with leukemia at the early age of 7. He became weaker and weaker. I took him to the beach the last day, and lifted his weak body out of the back seat, and knew for sure he would never get to go to the shore again. The next day he died, after waiting for the whole family to finish their day.

He took his last breath after each of us had told him what he had meant to us. We cried so hard, and couldn't imagine a day without Baj. Shortly after Baj's passing Steve and I broke up.

Because Baj was the only dog that I had ever had, I didn't know what to do. I was so empty without him, and I would wander from room to room expecting that I would see him. I wanted Baj back.

My daughter wanted me to be open to adopting a puppy, and not necessarily a Rhodesian ridgeback.

In April, about 5 months after saying good-bye to Baj, my daughter called and said "Mom come with me, have an open mind, and let's look at these baby Labradors that are advertised in the local newspaper.

Reluctantly, I went. We looked, and I saw this adorable little black "runt of the litter"---very shy but with a glance that said' --"I know you, don't you know me?"

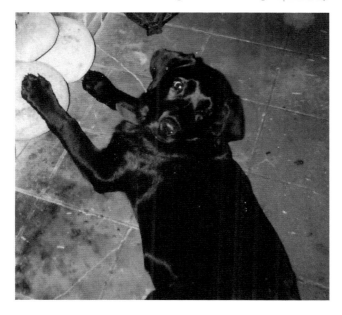

I went home, convinced that I was to wait for a
Rhodesian ridgeback. I had dreams about the little black
guy, at least three times.

Finally after three weeks of utter confusion, I called
the owner, and asked if there were any black labs left.
He said only one. If you want him you better come and
get him.

So, I did. My son John named him Rocky. The first
time we brought him in the house, he went laid and down
in the very spot where Baj had taken his last breath and
then looked at us as if to say "yes, I am back, and this is
my home." The house felt normal again.

When Rocky was three months old I took him for a
walk in Torrey Pines State Park where I would often go
to meditate with Baj, and where I buried Baj's ashes.
When Rocky and I got to the entrance of the park, Rocky
took off running as fast as he could. When I caught up
with him, he had started to dig up Baj's ashes. Rocky
turned and looked at me with such an intense stare --
as if to say "now do you know who I am?"

I smiled, and knew I had come to know and understand one of the best secrets on the planet. Animal souls do reincarnate. Rocky is now 11 years young and so passionately loved. He is my constant loving buddy, and the center of my heart.

Austin's Carbon Copy
Steve LaCounte

My dog Austin. White, a German shepherd, my best friend. 9 ½ years he was my companion. We ran, played, ate and he was my family. One day he became weak and fell, I knew something was wrong. As if in a postural state he lay motionless and stared into space.

My fears were realized with the meeting at the vet, cancer of the spleen. Advanced to the state of terminal. $2000.00 in diagnostic tests confirmed the news. My dog was dying. The vet's recommendation was to euthanize.

What the hell is that? Is he going to be made young again? Not the intention of the vet. No thank you!! I will take Austin home.

He lies on a blanket and looks up to me, am I dying? I know the answer but I can't let him know. As the spleen contracts, his gums pink up and he is able to stand and walk again.

Oh God he's o.k.! Two days he is as if nothing is wrong. My Austin is back, no sign of disease. Sheila my wife, goes to her friend's house and visits, I am now alone with my best friend, Austin.

The morning comes and we play as usual. The ball, the toy, and just sitting. Night time falls and my boy and I go to sleep on the living room floor. As the sun shines in through the window, I awake, where is Austin? I find him at the bottom of the stairs, laying there, with the look of help me on his face.

Unable to move and defecated, he looks at me and if he could speak, he would say, "Dad I'm sorry I messed on the carpet. I broke into tears saying, its o.k. boy you couldn't help it.

I knew the end was coming closer. So did Austin. I petted him and tried to make him feel better, but I was feeling worse. I told him just to try really hard and push all that blood engorging his spleen, back into his circulatory system.

His gums began to pink up a bit but he still couldn't muster the strength to move. I pulled him outside by the patio, so he could watch me put up the canopies over the hot tub and grilling area. He always loved to be with me when we cooked on the grill.

Then Austin began to vomit, over and over he wretched and suddenly his eyes rolled back in his head and he lay motionless. I ran over to him and said "don't die, don't die"! Austin try hard to stay! He took a breath and his eyes centered. Oh God you're o.k. His gums and tongue were as gray as it could get. I knew that he was not perfusing and that his spleen had distended once again.

I went into the house and got him some more water, but every time he drank he vomited. Lying there again he looked at me with almost no strength in his eyes and watched me work on the patio cover once more. The sun was moving so I pulled Austin over around the side of the tree into the shade. He couldn't even lift his head, so I stroked it and told him it was o.k.

Returning from the house with a fresh drink of water for my boy, I walked out the door and saw Austin open his mouth and take the last gasp of air that would keep him alive. His head fell to the side and he was gone.

I touched him and then ran away, saying over and over "my doggie died, my doggie died". When I could bear to return, I picked him up and put him in a bassinette and brought him in the house. His toys were placed with him for his journey.

I didn't call my wife Sheila and tell her, but waited until she called me later that night. Time, space and what I called life seemed to stop. I spent the night alone for the first time in nearly 10 years. As the dawn broke, I realized that it was indeed true, not just a cold, cruel dream, my friend, my companion, and the one who loved me no matter what was gone. A broken heart? No. A removed heart.

The preparations for Sheila to see him when she returned home, the preparations for burying my boy, and the thought that my parents were coming in from Tucson the next day and would see him not alive were more than I could take.

Twenty five years as a Paramedic / Firefighter, with death and dying all around me never prepared me for what I was now going through. As the next two days unfolded, Sheila came home, my parents arrived, and my dog, my friend, my boy, was sealed in a concrete box and placed in the ground.

Life is no longer the same. Trips out the back door, cooking on the grill, where Austin always got a sample of the meat, licking the food plates, an empty place on the couch, and the worst of all, there was no smiling face and waging tail looking out the front window when we drive down the driveway.

Life is now an empty place, void of the love and companionship that we have had. As the days pass I continue to cook on the grill and give Austin his piece. The little sample of the meat is placed on the ground over his resting place, and I say "here's your piece boy".

When I return the next day, the meat is gone. I say, "Was it good"?

I know that the ants really ate it, but in my mind I feel that I am still taking care of my doggie.

As many people believe, there is an afterlife for humans, be it reincarnation, heaven, or many other things that take place after death.

Many days pass and I feel no better. I feel that Austin is still with me and I feel him "talking" to me. Is there a possibility that there IS some sort of afterlife for my dog? Is he speaking to me from some other place? Is this the end? Do I just want there to be something more than just death?

Being brought up as a "Christian" I was taught to believe that we as humans go someplace after death. As I grew older and more educated, I rejected those thoughts and beliefs. Based on scientific evidence, I could no longer fall for the religious dogma.

So, when my boy died I began an extensive search for the "spirit" the "soul" or whatever a canine might have. I felt that Austin was "trying to reach out from the grave".

Is this just because I wanted to believe? Was it because now that I was confronted with death that I was willing to accept something that I had no proof of when it came to human afterlife? I have had several friends die and there has been no feeling of life reaching out from the grave. Why is it different now?

After many days of computer searching, I came upon a site by Brent Atwater. I read on her book about pet reincarnation. Was I falling for something stupid because of emotional loss or was there some truth to this?

I spent several days looking on the internet for a white German shepherd. I felt that Austin was reaching out to me and saying "come find me", "bring me home" Am I delusional? Am I caught up in some "cult" of dog reincarnation?

I found a person selling white German Shepherds in Shreveport LA I called him and made an appointment for that day to travel to Shreveport.

I felt that I was on a quest to find Austin. Sheila was at work so I left alone with a picture of Austin by my side. Sixty five miles to Shreveport.

When I arrived at the address, there were two men sitting in the front fenced in yard. I asked them if they were the people I had talked to about the white shepherds. They answered yes, and took me in a house that smelled of excrement, urine, and uncared for animals.

In a 6 x 6 cage in a bedroom there were approximately 12 puppies. I should have turned and left, but didn't. There were 6 black and tan and 6 white puppies. All had fleas and ticks and most had mange.

He opened the cage door and all ran from the cage and began to pee and defecate on the floor, all but one. One stayed in the cage, in the corner, and began to climb up and whine at me. He refused to leave.

I walked to the front of the cage opening and he ran over to me whining and wanted to have nothing to do with the others. Covered with fleas, I picked him up. Our eyes met and I knew there was something different happening.

I put him down in the middle of the other 6 black and 5 white puppies and he immediately ran away from them and back to me. Going against my better judgment, based on the condition and health of the dogs, I paid the guy and left with my new puppy, covered with fleas, ticks and a small amount of mange. I drove directly to our vet. $180 dollars later, we returned to our home.

Something was strange. When the new puppy entered the house I put him down, he walked down the hall to where Austin's water bowl should have been to look for water. This puppy knew the layout of the house. He went to the back door and whined to go out. It was if he had been in the house before.

I called Brent and she answered the phone. After several minutes of background history, I needed to address my skepticism and concerns.

This new puppy was born two and a half weeks before Austin died. So how could it be the "spirit" of Austin? She explained what she had written in her book.

There were, just like she said, all the tell tale signs. Austin never wanted to ride in our van, but about 3 weeks before he died he started going to the van and wanting to get in. We took him on several rides, which he enjoyed, this was a mystery to us, it was like a different dog emerging.

Austin started to get into our pool about 3 weeks before he died, this was something he was afraid to do all his life. At about the same time he began to "change". He just acted different, as if he was experiencing something new. After talking with Brent, it was clear that Austin had been "preparing" to leave.

As the days passed we began to notice that the new puppy was acting like Austin. He knew every room of the house, he found the toys that were Austin's, and it was like a clone!

We named him Carbon. What!? Carbon is black!   No. Carbon Copy!!

The most remarkable thing was when we looked inside his mouth and his tongue. Austin had a black spot on his tongue. Carbon has a black spot on his tongue.

The position of the black spot was only about ½ inch closer to the center on Carbon.

Carbon was jumping in the pool! It finally made sense. I am Austin and I am home!! I am different, and I want to do all those things I was afraid to do before. I also want to do all those things that I did before.
Come on Dad, let's have fun again!

After 2 years Austin and Carbon are here. As if born with a new healthy and young body, Austin is here through Carbon, Carbon eats with us, sleeps on our bed, goes everywhere with us.
Am I still sad? Yes.
Do I still miss the 10 year old dog Austin? Yes.
But I see Austin in everything that Carbon does.
Austin, you are home! Enjoy your new years of life, for we are together again.

Friend's 5 Reincarnations

My first dog Sunday was named for the day we got her. She was the little bitty beige one that wiggled out of the clustered puppies to adopt me. She was so tiny that I had to cradle her in my arms to protect her on our ride home.

She was my beloved companion through childhood and adolescence. We slept like cuddled littermates and grew up together. Who knew that wet puppy kisses from over a shoulder and toe fur in your face in the morning would be adorable, or that playing tug of war to get the best position under the bedspread would become a nightly ritual after our "treat?"

Although Sunday Dog was not a service or assistance dog, we established a bond and familiar patterns that wove our lives together. We developed routines, habits and special games just she and I knew.

Do car windows come without nose prints or furniture and clothes without "love fur" keepsakes? Not in our home!

Sunday taught me how to play. She taught me kindness, patience and tolerance. With her steadfast big brown eyes she taught me that temper tantrums and yelling are unacceptable, and that all-encompassing loving hugs and understanding solve everything.

Every day when I walked home from elementary school, there was Sunday sitting on the side of the street in front of our house patiently awaiting my arrival. One day a car accidentally ran over her. She still managed to be there with a crushed foreleg, multiple cuts and bruises holding on until I came home. She always followed my bike to the ice cream parlor and enjoyed her share while sitting on the steps beside me. Many times, I would get Sunday her own cone! She liked vanilla best!

One of her favorite things was to ride in the back of my Dad's boat to ensure that I was protected while we were skiing and swimming.

MAY · 59

SEP · 59

Sunday's friendship sustained and comforted me through life's emotional traumas and teenage boyfriends, as she listened with
a cocked head and understanding pricked ear.

She was never more than a heartbeat away.

Her watchful loving eyes guarded over my being and no one was admitted to our world without her consent

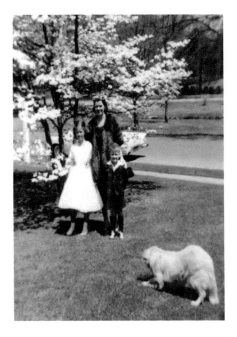

We sang and danced together to celebrate what I considered triumphs.

When I was happy she was. When I was sad, she would lie very quiet and still and look into the depths of my soul with her heartfelt protective gaze.

Sometimes she'd put a cold nose in my lap or a single paw on me just to let me know that she was there for me.

On the day I graduated from high school, Sunday suddenly, unexplainably collapsed in our driveway.

The veterinarian diagnosed advanced colon cancer and felt it was in her best interest to be euthanized. She meant the world to me.

My soul had to be there for and with her, as she had been for me.

I gathered her favorite "bankie and boo boos," and carefully, lovingly and tenderly placed her with them.

I held her in my arms as her trusting eyes focused on my face.   She listened to my heart's song while she tolerated the injection that sent her to heaven.

My heart died when hers stopped beating.

Years passed.

I couldn't find and was devoid of any unconditional
connection
like the one that I had with my Sunday Dog
who did not know she wasn't a "person," probably why
my relationship's breakup was easier than I imagined.

I was soul lonely.

I didn't know what an animal or interspecies
communicator was, but I kept seeing her alive and well in
my dreams.
Sometimes she was represented in another dog form
and didn't look like herself,
but I inherently knew it was her.

I could feel her with me.

Two more years passed
while I searched myriad litters of puppies to no avail.
My heart ached.
I felt my life though busy, was hollow.

Out of the blue,
from the hundreds of ads that I had half-heartedly read
since she died,
a particular newspaper classified caught my eye.

I drove to the house that Sunday afternoon
preparing to be disappointed again.

It's not that the puppies I interviewed weren't cute or
smart; I just knew that unexplainable
"something"
was missing!

I played with the fat male that waddled toward me
and scooped up several others
while constantly shoving, pushing away and
stepping over
the annoying little runt that determinedly
sat by my ankle no matter what I was doing
as if I was "her person."

I took my time making my decision.
When I notified the owner which pup I wanted,
he informed me that the only one left was the runt.
I was determined to go home with a dog.

I begrudgingly paid for the scruffie ivory colored fur ball
that the Universe had dealt,
I thought,
to my slow choice making.

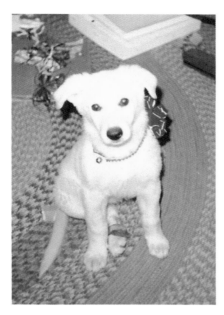

When I reluctantly and finally picked her up to examine what I paid for, her eyes talked to me in a way that resonated to my soul's core.

I felt a sense of "home" return to our household again.

Electra more rapidly than normal joined my daily routine as if it were old times and she had been there before.
How could this be I thought?
My heart sang again.

She participated in and over French fries, in helping me make all my major life decisions. She was wise beyond her years, understood everything we talked about and knew how to handle every life event.   Electra stabilized my life and kept me sane during my most trying times!
We went through a divorce; several job related moves, heartworm treatments and life's numerous ups and downs. She never left my side.

Even if I was floating in the chair at the lake, she would swim out to join me.

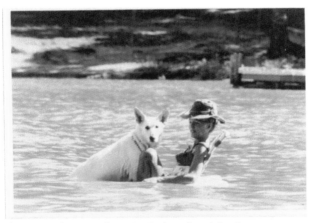

Electra took care of, protected and watched over everyone!

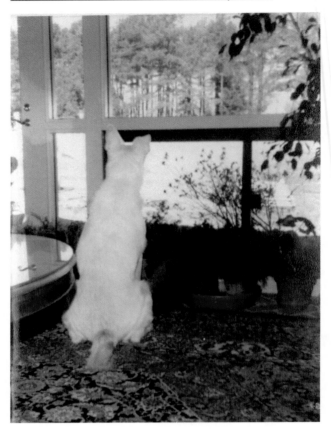

Electra was my second skin, my shadow, my "child."
We were connected by our very breath, telepathic
thought, heartbeat and soul. She set the standard for all
to follow: thoughtful, wise, kind, gentle, playful, SMART!
and would have given her life to save mine.

As her time was nearing, I would often see her
silhouetted against the terrace doors staring outside,
as if she was memorizing her earthly surroundings.

"I'm Home!" a Dog's Never Ending Love Story

When she died in her sleep of old age, a part of me died
with her.

I awoke bolt upright in the middle of the night
inherently knowing she had crossed the Rainbow Bridge.

Everything inside of me against all common sense,
felt she would never leave me and that we would be
reunited.

Though her body left, I ran with her spirit in my mind and
could feel her on my bed at night just before I went to
sleep.
 Often I saw her out of the corner of my eye
or felt her as a cool tingly nudge on my hand.

I told no one!
I **knew** inside my heart that I was not crazy.

My friends thought I was misguided and had "lost it" when I was intent on finding a dog "that had Electra's energy."

They were unaware of animal reincarnation and thought I was being absurd about the fact that Electra's spirit might return like I had read that humans do.

When I considered consulting a pet psychic, that idea brought responses from my friends like "what are you thinking, have you lost your mind?"

I just kept praying, hoping and searching…………..

There were other wonderful dogs that shared life with me between reincarnations. It was different looking into their eyes; you didn't experience that special soul connection that you "know" in your gut with your reincarnated pet.

My "love bug" "handsome fella," the "Boo Bear," "smart as can be" cute little Polka Dot, the Tweedle Dee and Tweedle Dum sisters, Orestes, loving "kind hearted" Blessing or elegant and picky Noysekophf and KT were all very special to me. I deeply love them all!
We shared many heartfelt memories; like finding a SOAKING WET tennis ball as a "gift" on my pillow one night.

Seven years later at a most inopportune time, my soul was relentless in creating a craving for a puppy. I made a few bogus calls to placate my inner persistence.

A few nights later about 6:30 a message on my answering machine stated: "I heard you wanted a red and white Border collie puppy. We had a litter of six, unbeknownst to us the Mother dog took them outside and five of them froze. If you want the one that survived, I'll sell him cheap since he has good bloodlines, but he may be brain damaged." Everything inside me said bad circumstances and go get that puppy!

At 10:30 pm on a Sunday night in 8 inches of snow in a MacDonald's parking lot, 5 week old "Friend" became mine.

When I looked into Friend's eyes, I just "knew" we had been together before. We bonded instantaneously! His training was incredibly easy.

At 6 weeks of age he almost immediately did everything my other dogs had done, including their quirky special loveable habits like "discussing" everything. He put up with my "I love you, yes I do" songs and baby talk, and made noises back to me. From 8 weeks on, he understood all my moods and hardly ever missed the meaning of what I was communicating. He was quite the "talker" and "singer" too. We were a duet that would make you laugh. We had a great Christmas routine!

We communicated with each other with our eyes. From the beginning, this puppy knew exactly where the toys that I had saved were kept, and he slept in the same position in the same bed spot as my other soul dogs had done.

For 17.5 years Friend was my "baby dog," guardian, playmate, best friend, co-worker, partner, confidant and teacher. We were inseparable. He was the love of my life! He was my everything!

He activated my spiritual side and taught me about a soul's contract (that I actually had one). At 15.5 he slipped on a slick floor while rounding a corner, fell and became paralyzed. The veterinarian advised euthanasia stating "he had lived a good long life."

I was NOT ready to let him go!

I inherently KNEW he was not ready to go!

After many many long soul bearing, begging and pleading talks with God and even more heartfelt tearful prayers, Friend's plight activated my abilities as a medical intuitive and medical intuitive diagnostician.

I could look at him and see inside his body. I could see his broken vertebrae, and see where his spinal cord nerves were damaged. I knew about his nose infection and his diminished lung function before the doctor would tell me. It was a frightening awakening of my gifts, yet Friend had chosen to experience this entire ordeal in order to be my spiritual teacher.

Friend's medical predicament induced me to search, research, and to eventually believe and trust in holistic, integrative and alternative therapies of energy medicine and energy healing.

His "accident" expanded my awareness beyond current traditional medical limitations and mindsets.

The doctors told me Friend would never walk again. My soul knew otherwise!

Friend was the first dog ever to be released from the NC State University School of Veterinary Medicine hospital on a breathing machine because his oxygen values were approximately 55. According to them, due to his fall, Friend would never breathe on his own.

I prayed for guidance to know how to heal him.
I worked with him for months, praying, being guided and learning how to heal him.

120 days after his accident Friend walked into the veterinarian school's hospital on his own and with no oxygen assistance for his last check up. His oxygen blood levels were now within normal range.

His vertebrae, discs and spinal cord nerves were restored. Friend's healing results were documented by X-rays, blood work and pulmonary test results.His final release stated "We don't know what you did, but keep it up. We wish Friend all the best."

Friend walked and had a wonderful quality of life for 2 more years.

    Thanks to Friend's journey, my new life as a medical intuitive and energy healer began.   I honor and celebrate all of his contributions to my life and for all the things that he taught me for the benefit of others. God bless my spiritual guide and master teacher Friend!

When my human soul mate/twin flame was unexpectedly and suddenly killed in a car crash, Friend was there to console me and "talk" about everything. I buried my tears in his luxurious ruff. He is a part of my life journey and always and forever etched and ingrained into my heart, soul and a part of my being. He taught me to know reincarnation with a soul pet is reality.

As Friend drew his last breath resulting from kidney failure, staring into my eyes, I knew that his soul would return. Even during my greatest anguish, for the first time my heart understood patience.

I knew that I would "know" when he replaced his old and ill body with a new one in order to come home to me.

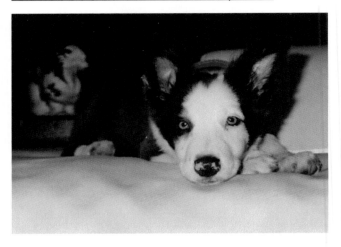

I chose Electra as a companion for Friend while he was aging. She eagerly bounced in and out of our lives with hugs, kisses, wet tennis balls, wiggling unbridled curiosity and endless "wide open" energy for nonstop walks.

They always slept together, and seeing them sleep on their backs with feet nonchalantly and indiscriminately splayed wide open to expose tummies to the warm sun, was one of my favorite memoires!

Everyone said "there's something 'special' about that dog." I knew why. When she sang her "woo woo" song to greet people, she was my precious little "squirrel girl," "Miss Personality!" Every morning we would choose THE perfect bandana from her extensive collection of multiple styles and color choices. Some days required several wardrobe changes to suit each special occasion.

Electra was stunned and scared the day she and Mikey sniffed his cold body; it was as if she sensed that Friend had passed the torch for her to take care of "Mommy." The old dog had trained her well.

I now understood the difference between a soul connected dog like Friend was, and a wonderful pet like Electra.

It was a transformative experience for me when months later Friend's spirit "walked in" to Electra's life form. He taught me about another level of consciousness that I had not known throughout his previous incarnations.

Friend showed me that a soul, who had previously died, can "walk into" an existing body, a concept that I had never even considered before that time.

Electra not only maintained her own personal qualities, she now embodied and exhibited the added personality, behavior traits and preferences of Friend. Their two spirits had combined in Electra's body!

We bonded at a level of closeness that I had not known before. She knew my next move before I did! We read each other's minds, yet we always discovered wonderful new surprises to share between us.

She was a happy very intense little girl and her smile made my heart smile. I felt safe, special, comforted and loved in her presence. Her joy and eagerness to experience each day with a renewed curiosity was infectious and uplifting. She taught me to reappreciate lots of things that had become mundane in my life.

As she grew older, sometimes after "work" we would sit in front of my computer and preview puppy sites for hours. She would stand with her paws on the desk and look intently at the computer screen so I could get her approval on which sites had the best red and white Border collie litters.

Instinctively and sadly I knew we were practicing for a future event. I promised Electra that when it was time, I would choose from the site that she was most attentive to in our searches.

Our relationship embraced 13 wonderful magical years until mammary cancer took her gorgeous mahogany body. Her spirit did not want to leave me; I ached for her not to depart.

Although she fought hard, her body was beyond staying. I honored that horrible and painful fact.

Whenever I leave my dogs, I have always put on my reddest lipstick and kissed them on the forehead, to symbolize my love always surrounding and protecting them while we were apart.

As she left,

I knew her energy would return
because she would not say goodbye.

She was still taking care of <u>me</u>
when her eyes permanently closed.

Once again my soul shattered!

God, how I miss her!

I still cry for her in my heart.....

For years after Friend's and Electra's passing, I'd find
a memory filled toy or hear familiar sounds in
another room. At times, my cats seemed to be
paying attention to an imaginary "friend."
I continually consoled myself during my depression
and crying bouts by watching "our" favorite website's
puppy images.

Each loss of my soul pet had gotten more painful.
It seemed that the older I became,
the worse the pain was.
When I would force myself forward to procure a puppy,
each time that I would call about the one I picked,
it had just been sold.
One exasperated breeder that I had contacted too late
too many times, stated, "perhaps you should send a
deposit"
to which I responded,
"When its time I'll know."

I watched endless months
that turned to even more years
of weekly photos, daily puppy updates,
videos and rescue webcams.

Nothing!

I really didn't even care because my heart still mourned to my core. I also didn't want to feel hurt this bad again.

However, I kept being compelled to continue watching puppy updates and checking all the sites and shelters no matter how upset they made me.

Then, one day while watching Electra's favorite site,
this fluffy little red and white fur ball in motion,
dragging a LARGE stuffed toy in his mouth ran gleefully
zoom-zoom-zoom across my computer screen.

My heart unexpectedly started pounding,

my stomach squenched up
and tears welled up in my eyes.

I frantically bookmarked the video.

I must have watched, rewatched, cried and rewatched
and
memorized that video hundreds of times!!!

I could feel that puppy in my soul!

I called the owner to check his status. He was available albeit 2500 miles away. I thought, "3.5 hours on a plane, TOO far to fly the little fellow with stopovers."

Who knows why, but I was compelled to call a second time to recheck the flight schedules. Unbeknownst to me the Universe had arranged for the airline carrier to add an extra holiday nonstop flight from the Midwest area to our airport.

Now I had no excuses not to get him! I had been unencumbered for years and a new pup, well......................
I talked to and questioned the puppy's guardian till she was probably really tired of me. In one conversation, she jokingly referred to him as "bad boy." I asked why.

She stated that he had a fabulous personality, was "quite the talker" and had, "a strange white marking on his right hip."

She said she would send me more of his newborn photos and other pictures so I could see the unusual white marking.

The image took my breath away and sent chills up my spine and all my friends into a chorus of "what don't you get?"

This pup had already been assigned to me by a higher level than any of us knew at that time. It was as if God commissioned an Angel to paint a monogram of my signature on this puppy's hip so I would **clearly** understand that he was meant to be mine!

With a weary heart, afraid and excited I met him at the airport, VERY apprehensive! I had never picked an unhugged puppy before from just photos and videos, much less from a distance.

What if I had the wrong pup and we didn't connect?

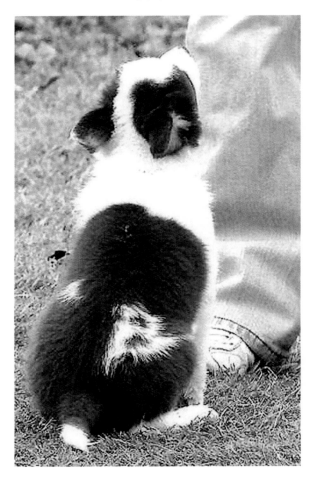

I carefully tiptoed up to the huge beige crate so
I wouldn't startle the tiny reddish brown puppy huddled
in a corner inside. When I unlatched the door, he
launched out of that crate and immediately sat all 7
pounds of 9 weeks old mahogany fluff right down in front
of me. He looked up and stared directly into my eyes as if
to say "where have you been? Now let's get on with our
life!"

I knew his name would be "My Best Friend." Then he
scrambled onto my lap. That warm new puppy smell filled
the car while he slept in the fold of my arm all the way
to my house that had now become our home.

He responded to his "old" name without missing a beat. He <u>knew</u> where his bed was, recognized his past life toys and regathered them into his same toy spot where they were supposed to be! He did not even inspect the new toys, he wanted HIS toys! He talks, carries on great discussions, sings, and does all the things all my other soul dogs "did."

When I look into his eyes we never left one another. He is my "baby dog," my forever best Friend.

When my heart asked where you have been, his spirit replied: I had to exchange my old body for this new one so I could be in your life again.

At 10 weeks old with one perfect white tipped pricked ear and a random VERY creative expressive one,
Friend knew and responded to my old dog's commands.
No major training was necessary, just "reminders."
And can he ever "work" those blue and gold eyes and his gold "cheekies" to get almost anything he wants!

Wherever I am, he is! He jumps right in or wedges his pink brown nose into EVERY thing to investigate or participate in what I'm doing!
New Friend "back talks" and "discusses" many directives that I give. If he doesn't like something, he has a vast repertoire of "talking" sounds to let me know he is NOT happy with my command or what is going on.
We've discussed and STILL discuss "stay" or "no" MANY times!

Friend's rendition of Electra's "woo woo" song is a hoot! He even has ME trained to fetch his ball from under the furniture or out of the pond!

He's my old adult dog with few puppy moments except he moves at "full throttle - wide open," and is learning how to operate this body's new feet.

You can tell he's awake because he's chewing! Can "tuggies," "chewies," smelly toys, soggy balls and "Mr. Bears" strewn ALL OVER my once clean house, and incessant, I mean INCESSANT squeaky toys be truly adorable? When he's quiet, I worry!

Even Mikey our senior cat recognizes this 90 day reincarnate. She lived with first Friend and Electra. She slept on first Friend's grave for the longest time.

It was like a class reunion. Mikey knew they knew each other from before, but they didn't know how to act now. Mikey instigated head bumps, a game of tag with a playful paw bat, and she nonchalantly weaves back and forth under Friend's stomach before eating dinner together and then cleaning his face and ears.

They can be seen intertwined in the late afternoon sun napping, or haggling for space on my bed's pillow each night. She settles more and more easily into second place as he grows. Sometimes Mikey exasperated by "His Puppyhood," has to "explain it" with a swipe of her claw to inspire respect for his feline buddy.

When Friend does a major "no no," (like teething on an antique or marking new territory), I'm momentarily willing to give him away free to anyone. Then he slinks down the hall tail between his legs with that B illuminated brightly against his mahogany fur, My heart melts.

I sing this to "His Puppyhood" when he has been V E R Y naughty:

"When I'm in doubt and want to throw you out,
I can clearly seeeeeeeeeeeeeeeee
With that big bright white B,
God made you 'specially for me! ☺"

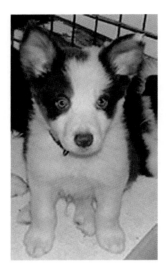

I feel blessed to have gentle paw pads stroking my face to awaken me each morning.
We share lots of bonding hugs. He's a "love machine!" and demands to be the center of attention (of course!)
Eventually Friend prods me with his cold wet nose, smelling of warm puppy breath insisting with very intense eyes, that I need to get up and feed him now!

Then he jumps off "our" bed and stands there barking until I comply! Each day as we grow older together, I'm continuously reminded that all the eccentric little habits, routines, traits, favorite toys, foods, spots and tricks known only to my soul and my "Sunday dogs," is back home with me in a non returnable "monogrammed" fur form named Friend!

In your darkest hours after transition, choose hope! Your pet might be just a heartbeat away!

Animal Reincarnation is REAL!!!

Just ask Friend,
the Dog with **my** "B" on His Bottom!
*Soon you'll feel **"I'm Home!"***

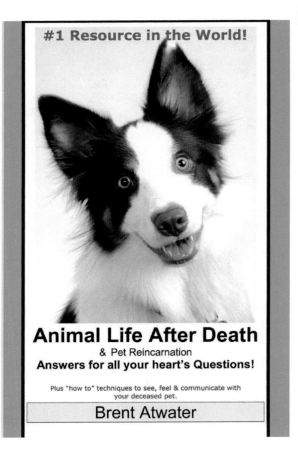

#1 Resource in the World!

Animal Life After Death
& Pet Reincarnation
Answers for all your heart's Questions!

Plus "how to" techniques to see, feel & communicate with
your deceased pet.

Brent Atwater

The following partial chapters and excerpts are
from Ms. Atwater's companion book
**Animal Life after Death
& Pet Reincarnation-**
Answers for all your hearts questions!

The Dog with a "B" on His Bottom!

My research began years and years ago when I lost my fiancé in an unexpected auto accident.
I desperately wanted to find him, so I started investigating ways that his energy could return to me.

While studying the reincarnation process, I became more and more aware that my dogs demonstrated similar if not downright exact character traits of each other.

"Friend" my border collie was born with a white "B"
on his bottom that exactly matched my signature.
I took that as my sign and mission to write about what
my heart had come to know to be true;
Pet Reincarnation is real!

While furthering my investigations and documenting
the evidence I was collecting, I gathered true stories from
around the globe. Each one taught me even more about
reincarnation and the animal kingdom. I read about live
pets that had reincarnated multiple times within each
owner's life, like Friend had done in mine. Others
validated and illustrated examples of each nuance of my
research.

I want the reader of my *"I'm Home!"* books to be
able to touch each animal whose story is in this book.
I want the reader to be able to talk to each pet's guardian
to hear "their story," so no one could say I "made this
stuff up!"

The *Animal Reincarnation* book represents insights
derived from reoccurring evidence found time and time
again and from all of the various questions asked in TV
and radio interviews, in workshops, lectures,
presentations and book signings that I have done and will
do.

Whenever I think that I have covered E-V-E-R-Y
question, another one comes along. I revise *Animal
Reincarnation* almost every year to reflect my latest and
most current knowledge base of questions and answers.
Based upon requests by readers, I add
new energy techniques to each revision.

It is my intent for **this book to empower you** to
communicate with and understand your pet's energy
before, during and after their reincarnation process.
That's also why I founded AMIDI, the process of how to
see and track your pet's life force energy from their
current life form, through their transition and into their
reincarnation evolution.

I was a non believer in all this "other side stuff" until
Mike's death showed me "all that is." Because I trusted
him in life, I trusted him in death to teach me what I now
share with you.

It is my intent to educate readers about the thought that animal reincarnation is a very real possibility and for those "having their own experience," a definite reality!

The History of Reincarnation

Reincarnation is believed to occur when the spirit or soul, after the death of the physical body, comes back to earth life in a new body.

The belief in Reincarnation dates back as far as the ancient Egyptians in addition to the Buddhist, Hindu, Jainism and Taoism religions. Simply put, to believe in reincarnation means you believe that the soul's life force energy is immortal i.e. ongoing and infinite.

Animal reincarnation is sometimes called transmigration; a process that the Hindu religion, Yogic view and others believe happens after someone dies. This process is about the belief that the spirit of the deceased person moves into the body of another person or animal.

The popular reincarnation belief is that when one's physical body dies their spirit is able to choose to be reborn into another body because the life force energy known as the "spirit" or "soul" is everlasting.

It's a common belief that the new body the old soul chooses to inhabit is based on its past life Karma and its karmic purpose or spiritual arrangement with you. To me, it's a reasonable expectation that many people would believe their pets will reincarnate. Although not all people believe in reincarnation; it's interesting that most people agree that you will be with all your pets when you die and cross to the other side.

In 2007 a respected British leading independent research company YouGov conducted a study and found that dogs proved to be the type of animal most likely to be considered reincarnated by pet owners: 51% said they had or have dogs that they believe reincarnated while 44% said their cat returned.

Some individuals, who have not experienced a reincarnated pet, feel that pets do not return because they have no need to or that the animals don't have lessons to learn.

Others who have not experienced a reincarnated angel animal suggest that a deceased loved one who passed may have sent you a special furry, finned or feathered baby to be with you. In my research and experience, animals reincarnate for diverse reasons.

A soul connected forever pet is usually a spiritual teacher, guide or guardian spirit that travels with you in pet form throughout your earthly journey.

The reincarnation information herein was researched and gathered from friends, clients, myriad stories and testimonials in addition to my personal experiences. We all believe that in my dog Friend's and each of our individual's pet's life and in whatever form they choose, animals DO reincarnate!

Use any information that resonates with you and remember-

There can always be exceptions!

When you've lost your beloved pet, service animal, companion animal, assistance dog, therapy pet, soul pet partner and forever finned, feathered or fur baby, - "love of your life," your "heart and soul and everything good in the world" "child," don't lose hope. Listen to your heart's urgings, watch your dreams and follow your soul's knowing. Because your pet is a part of the tapestry of your life and every fiber of your being, pay attention to your intuition and inner guidance.

If you feel that you want to or must hold onto your pet's beds, belongings and toys, there is a reason. Some part of your soul's inner being knows that they will be back.

Each and every animal's soul is a spirit composed of eternal life force energy that lives forever in our vast Universe. Whether or not it's your soul pet, forever fur baby, animal spirit guide or spiritual teacher in an animal form, God/ the Universe honors your pet's choice to reincarnate in whatever way to be with you in various physical bodies throughout your life time.

It's not **just** about your animal's soul's path or singular lessons. Your pet's simple reincarnation or other reincarnation structures such as a "walk in," "over soul" or "soul braid" is about what you have to accomplish **together**.

He/she will continue to reincarnate, "walk in," "soul braid" or "over soul" until your combined learning opportunities and spiritual agreements are fulfilled. Animal reincarnation is about the human animal soul arrangement that you each have made with one another for this and other lifetimes.

Know that your pet is never gone forever. He's just changed the form of his life force energy. Give your animal's life force energy time to recover, recalibrate, regenerate and to choose or relocate in a new body if they have agreed to return.

The reincarnation contract is not complicated. It's a simple soul agreement to return to you. The form of reentry and timing may create some twists and turns in the process but it's a simple soul to soul contract.

The actual process can be an effortless approach into a new body, have nuances of electromagnetic interfacing as seen in a soul braid or take a more drawn out approach like a walk-in's relocations during reentry. All of these potential forms of reincarnation accomplish the fact that your pet is back to share life with you.

Your heart will know when it's time to look for them again. Follow your heart, you can't miss them!

The Reincarnation premise: A simple concept!

If you boil WATER, what does it make? STEAM
If your freeze STEAM, what does it become?
ICE!
If you melt ICE, what does it become?
WATER!
And so the never ending energy cycle goes on!
Life force essential soul energy NEVER changes!
It just changes into different physical FORMS.

Think about the water- ice- steam concept!

Physical Death is the Beginning:

Each physical body provides an opportunity to depart whether it ages, is physically broken, ill, just wears out or opts out early, in a birth or newborn process. It's part of the trading spaces process.

Due to shorter life spans, upgrading to a healthier body is a necessity for our beloved animals, birds, fish or reptiles so they can continue sharing your life's journey.

If you are reading this book prior to the impending passage of the "love of your life," KNOW that death and transition is the **first** step in reuniting with you. This fact will help you during the transition and waiting process. Keep reminding yourself of that thought! It will save a lot of tears if you wait in anticipation and not grief.

The Transition Process:

During the transition process, your pet's physical body will be in conflict with its soul's love for you and wanting to stay with you in your current situation. Oftentimes when a pet is preparing to pass and you subliminally want them to "hang on" for your sake:

> The pet will walk away from you,
> Not look at you in your eyes,
> Avoid their normal personal contact with you,
> Stay or hide in another room trying to avoid
> your conflicting energy.

Another sign of impending transition is when you see an older or sickly pet sitting at a window or door staring out as if they are memorizing their last earthly view. They are!

During the death process do not have any guilt. Whatever occurred was "scripted" and agreed upon between your souls before it happened. Your pet knew and knows he was/ is loved and that you were/are doing the best you could/can do. If the death was "an accident" that scenario was planned before they came to be with you in this incarnation. KNOW that everything is exactly as it should have been for the lessons and learning opportunities you each contracted to experience.

Signs that Physical Transition is Imminent:

Before or during the timeframe when your pet starts withdrawing its life force energy, which is usually 24 – 48 hours prior to leaving its body, you can see its aura gradually diminish. During that time or beforehand you can ask your pet if it is going to reincarnate.

If you see auras (a field of subtle, luminous radiation surrounding a person, pet or object like a halo), you will be able to notice as your animal's electromagnetic life force energy becomes more centrally organized near the heart area. At that time an animal's physical body becomes colder throughout their entire system as their energy is being incrementally withdrawn in preparation for departure. This progressive physical process starts as cold paws and ears, pale gums, then lackluster or nonresponsive eyes, etc.

If you can track and see life force energy as I do, you will see an animal draw his aura energy inside of his body. You will then watch whirling purple energy rotating in an upward counter clock wise direction as the life force essence crosses the veils.

At the same time your pet's aura will appears as a black area with lots of holes in it. When the auric energy becomes totally black, you know the life force energy of your pet has completed transition and has detached from its body.

Affirmation to assist a pet's transition choice:

The affirmation below will assist your cherished companion in transitioning easier and without horrific physical complications.

1. Hold its front paws with your hands or place the hand that you write with (that's your energy sending hand) on the pet's body near its heart.

2. Look into your pet's eyes if possible but not necessary. Ask with your heart or voice out loud: (This can be said one time or as often as you wish.)

"Fill in blank with Pet's name, I love you.
I honor, respect and support your choices.
From the love in my heart, I send you my life force energy to use as you so choose."

Your intent with this specific declaration will assist in making your pet's transition as gentle as possible.   Do not change the wording or it will change the type of energy being sent.

It is imperative that you use the words **"as you so choose"** so your pet can use that additional energy boost provided from the love of your heart to either cross over or to get better--- Then it's THEIR choice!

An animal like a human has several predetermined exit point choices within their lifetime. Your pet can choose to survive and stay at this exit point or cross. That concept goes hand in hand with the phase about a cat's nine lives.

Remember, no matter what you desire, there is a point beyond which any physical body cannot regenerate or recover.

Usually after you have said this phrase, if your pet has decided to leave, at some point in time before they cross the Rainbow Bridge, your pet will create a tender *memory moment* as their way of acknowledging your love and releasing them to complete this incarnation's soul's path.

 A client's cat was extremely ill for months and stayed alone in her bed in a dark corner. Several days after the client started saying the affirmation above, her cat got up, came over to sit in her lap and purred for the first time since her illness began. Later that night she calmly went to sleep (unassisted) in the safe haven of her owner's love while her guardian was stating this affirmation.

Is it important to believe in reincarnation?

Yes. Your open minded energy facilitates the return of your pet more readily. Negative energy creates a barrier.

If you do not completely believe in reincarnation but might entertain the concept, hold the thought that "at least I'll give it a try, Why not?" Then your pet can come back more easily if it has chosen to do so. Otherwise your pet will not reincarnate to honor your free will thought process until you open your mind to the possibility of their return.

If you choose not to believe in reincarnation and your pet was scheduled to return in this lifetime, the Universe will provide many situations to assist you with an "opportunity" to change your mind in order for you to complete your spiritual agreement with your animal. Otherwise, you will need to complete your contract in another incarnation.

Prayers for Reincarnation:
When you want to ask your pet if it's going to reincarnate, hold its front paws with your hands or place your hand on the pet's body near its heart, look into its eyes if possible and ask with your heart or out loud:
I ask and it is my intent to know if we will be together again in this lifetime. Will you return to live with me again in this lifetime?
Your heart will hear the answer.
If you do not receive an answer, it may be due to the fact that your pet has not made their decision yet.

If you do not receive an answer that you feel is clear and factual due to the emotional upheaval that everyone is experiencing, then use the prayers set forth in a later section, to receive a response after your pet is on the other side.

Since I can see inside an animal's current body and see their future physical energy form, this gift allows me to determine when an animal is going to reincarnate and what they will look like! We teach our Animal Hope Counselors™ this skill so they can help heal hearts.

Grief:

Although physical death is so very heart wrenching and may seem permanent, you *must remember* that it is the FIRST step toward reincarnation. They need to shed that old body for a newer better version!

Since your beloved companion is so connected to you, chronic crying depletes your pet's regenerative energy and hampers their ability to transition back to you in the best and quickest way possible!

Give your "baby" permission to do **as they so choose**. Honor their journey's timeframe from death to relife so they can be a part of yours quicker! Although this is so hard to do in critical times, it's all about mutual love and respect.

Focusing your attention and emotions on the DEATH of your pet and being trapped in a never ending focus on a grief will slow down and repel your pet's reincarnation process!

Remember, Death is the **FIRST** step to coming back to you! When you free your mind of grief limitations, only then can your pet change its energy's direction and choose to come back.

Here's more !

How Many Times Can An Animal Reincarnate?
God Animals

Do Animals Have Other Soul Contracts?
Can a Pet Return as a Human?
Types of Reincarnations
How Long Does Reincarnation Take?

How to Communicate with Your Deceased Pet
How to see and feel your Deceased Pet

What Can Affect Communication with My Pet?

How Your Deceased Pet Contacts You
What can Prohibit My Pet from Visiting Me?
How Do We Get Back Together?
Recognition: How Will I Recognize My Pet?
and WONDERFUL Questions from the Audience!

Message to Book Clubs,
Professional Associations & Organizations

I'd be delighted to speak with you over the phone or schedule a presentation.
Please email me: Brent@BrentAtwater.com

*** and for Cat lovers!

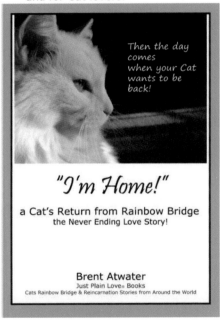

More Resources and Information on Animal Life after Death & Pet Reincarnation

1. Pet Loss Support- Ask questions in the World's # 1 Pet Loss, Animal life after death and Reincarnation Group on Facebook.

2. Blog: http://petreincarnation.blogspot.com

3. Events: Want an Event in your area, email us!

4. Newsletter on Animal Life after Death and Animal Communication

5 Radio Show: "Alive Again" on www.PetLifeRadio.com show

6. Return from Rainbow Bridge Poem and Videos

7. Memorial Wristband:
   Celebrate with a Reincarnation Wristband engraved: **My Love is Never Ending. I'm coming back to YOU!™** which can be found on our websites.

8. Animal Life After Death Cards- Inspirational quotes and cards that assist you on the journey from pet loss to healing!

 9. Share your stories on **Brent Atwater Pet Loss Facebook Fan Page** or email us.

a Dog's Return from Rainbow Bridge

When a Dog dies his Soul transitions to a special place in Heaven
called the Rainbow Bridge.
There He is alive and well, a part of Never Ending Love.
He is healed, whole, and restored.

He sniffs special friends, meets family and hugs loved ones.
They chase one another, play and bark together.
There is plenty of food, treats, chewies, balls, bones and sunshine.
Everyone is warm, safe and comfortable in their beds.

He visits you in dreams with memories of the special times you shared.
He is happy and content EXCEPT for one thing.
He misses that special bond with the person he had to leave behind.
He sends signs to let you know he is thinking about and watching over you.
His Soul is ALWAYS by your side.
He has NEVER stopped loving you!

Then the day comes when your Dog wants to be back.
There are promises to keep.
He wiggles and sparkles with intent.
It's time to return to Earth as you both have agreed.
His energy vibrates faster and faster,
forming a Heart to be loved.

He feels the pull of your Prayers and yearnings.
He is strengthened by the power of your belief in Never Ending Love.
Full of Hope and Faith he leaves the safety of Rainbow Bridge.
His Soul begins the search for the Haven of your heart.

In perfect timing that moment arrives.
You find one another!
Time stands still as you look into each other's Soul.

Your heart is etched with the feeling of recognition in his eyes.
Cautiously you move forward filling the gaps that complete your bond.
Your touch caresses his beloved velvet head.
All sadness is gone.
Your heart is whole again!

Your Dog has returned from the Rainbow Bridge.
Together you begin again,
another journey
in the Eternal Cycle of Life!
Your Love is here
Now,
Forever and Always!

Author: Brent Atwater
*****
Taken from Ms. Atwater's book Animal Reincarnation: Animal Life after Death-
Everything You Always Wanted to Know! Video also available
Translated into many languages
5/5/13

Return from Rainbow Bridge

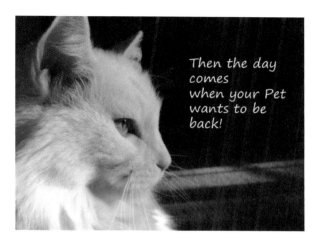

Then the day comes when your Pet wants to be back!

Return from Rainbow Bridge Videos
in 10+ languages at
http://www.youtube.com/user/BrentAtwater

Return from Rainbow Bridge Poems
Download and print out in YOUR language at
www.justplainlovebooks.com

Return from Rainbow Bridge Facebook page
Please share with your friends. Pass the love and
awareness forward!

Return from Rainbow Bridge Memorials When
your pet comes "home," we'll create a certified RRB
Memorial and Feature you on our Return from Rainbow
Bridge Facebook Fan page in your native language. Here
are a few samples:

The Global Pet Loss Hope!™ Initiative

"Turning Pet Loss Heartbreak into Joy!"
The Global Pet Loss Hope & Healing! ™ Initiative -
"Turning Pet Loss Heartbreak into Joy!" was launched by
Brent Atwater to ignite hope and expand awareness for
those suffering from the devastating death of a pet. Ms.
Atwater's decades of animal reincarnation research and
her weekly Q & A radio shows illuminated the
extraordinary need for perspectives beyond current pet
loss grief support viewpoints.

Ms Atwater states, "Research has proven that pets are an
intimate part of most families and a beneficial healthy
addition to people's lives. Pet Loss is an ongoing part of
the human life cycle. The need has never been greater to
address the positive side of pet loss for well being.
Raising consciousness re: animal reincarnation helps
uplift emotional suffering during pet bereavement and
ignite hope by offering a healing spiritual perspective that
stops the perpetuation of "my pet is gone forever" grief.

What is an Animal Hope Counselor™?
Current pet loss counseling and the "coping with pet loss"
process focuses on grief, condolences and memorials.
Animal Hope Counselors™ concentrate on positive
spiritual perspectives that ignite hope.

The perception that pet loss is permanent is a limited
awareness when dealing with bereavement options. Relife through animal reincarnation; a belief held since 3000
BC and the Egyptian era that is embraced by some of the
world's oldest and largest religions.

AHCs use traditional bereavement counseling techniques
in addition to bringing an awareness of death that
illuminates the integral human animal bond of spiritual
agreements, ongoing animal communication and pet's
soul contracts.

What is a Pet Loss Hope™ Ambassador?

Losing your pet is a heartbreaking experience beyond compare. It's psychologically sound to address and support a person's emotional distress after pet loss with trained animal bereavement counselors and through professional therapy and techniques.

It is unhealthy however to totally embrace a "mending" attitude that relies only on pet death grief as the sole focus while discouraging or not presenting any alternative viewpoints for a person to consider.

The prevailing pet loss support atmosphere is about "emotionally working through your pain." It's more about "recovery" rather than empowering discovery! Animal grief counselors seem to center on dealing with pet death strife and overcoming grief with therapy to "get you through."   PLHAs offer uplifting educational materials and revitalizing personal experiences that encourage and support an individual to question their perspectives and consider a wider awareness.

Pet Loss Hope Ambassadors™ come is a variety forms. The pet guardian who has experienced the joy of animal reincarnation and is living with their reincarnated pet is the highest level! This person has lived through all of the stages of their pet's transition over the Rainbows Bridge, the "am I crazy?" self-questioning, the incessant searching for reconnection and then reuniting with their soul pet in perfect timing under Universal "coincidences."

A PLHA is not a designation bestowed only to an individual. Any company, manufacturer, institution, Trust, 501(c) organization, educational or healthcare facility, book store, well-being or spiritual center, local veterinarian, homeless rescue shelter or pet sitting service and many more can choose to address pet death with a positive spin that ignites healing with hope! It's an understanding or knowing that animal reincarnation is a revitalizing truth and a pet's NEVER ending love story!

Brent Atwater- Animal Communicator

The world's Authority on
Animal Life after Death & Reincarnation
Pioneer & Founder- AMIDI the field of Animal Medical
Intuitive Diagnosis™

Brent Atwater and "Friend" the dog with a "B" on his Bottom are the world's leading pet loss, animal life after death and reincarnation.

Ms. Atwater has the extraordinary gift to see inside a body to accurately diagnose current and future issues. At age 5 Brent's intuitive talents were discovered by Duke University's Dr. J B Rhine the founder of ESP in his initial investigations.
Ms. Atwater's specialized intuitive diagnostic abilities have earned her the nickname of the "human MRI."

Her Medical Intuitive practice has highly respected, evidence based, documented and published case studies. Brent can see the organs, nerves, bones, tissue et al inside your body, plus diagnose and predict future events. Therefore Ms. Atwater can determine if and when your pet is going to reincarnate and what they will look like!

Brent's healing work regenerating her dog's spinal cord nerves and vertebra has been documented by NC State University's School of Veterinary Medicine. She has been a speaker and teacher for the NC Veterinary Association and taught at the New York Open Center. For decades Ms. Atwater has pioneered and founded AMIDI the field of Animal Medical Intuitive Diagnostic Imaging™. Her Medical Intuitive Diagnosis MIDI and AMIDI books are groundbreaking resource books for the science of Medical Intuition and Healing Animals with Integrative Energy Medicine.

In 1987 Brent founded the *Just Plain Love®* Charitable Trust. After law school and the death of her fiancé, Brent refocused her career on helping pets and their people heal. Ms. Atwater has authored 10 *Just Plain Love®* Books with more to follow.

Ms. Atwater has devoted decades to researching animal life after death, pet reincarnation and human animal spiritual contracts which produced multiple books whose titles are translated into other languages.

Brent is a true animal lover who offers us the benefit of her incredible gifts and her passion to help heal and uplift the lives of pets and their people! Her mission is to ignite hope and healing in people after pet loss in addition to activating and empowering every person's inherent abilities and Gifts.

Ms. Atwater is also a pioneer in healing art medicine by scientifically documenting the healing energy, diagnostic abilities and healing benefits of her art for healthcare *Paintings That Heal®* (www.BrentAtwater.com). She is one of the contemporary American painters who are bringing forth a new cultural renaissance by blending her classical artistic training with spirituality and energy infused into her healing art.

Brent's *Just Plain Love® Books,* weekly ASK Brent radio shows, podcasts, blogs, invigorating and inspiring audience participatory workshops (with awesome demonstrations), upbeat seminars, speaking tours, presentations and consultations bring about transformative and positive results.

"Friend" is the co-host of the Animal life after Death & Reincarnation shows. He is a Red tri colored Border collie. Friend "B"elieves his mission is to expand awareness about animal reincarnation to help heal hearts. When he's not assisting Brent with paw signings, pet fund raising events or practicing hugs and kisses for his pet therapy work, Friend enjoys being spoiled, herding fish and turtles in his pond and playing with his "Mister Bears."

The Just Plain Love® Story

"Experiencing a pediatric intensive care, oncology, burn or trauma unit to me, is a heart wrenching jolt to anyone's world. I had to summon all my "heart" to handle the various states of disrupted life. Right then and there I decided that a positive Light needed to shine on the hearts and minds of these struggling little souls, so new to earth and so old to the diseases, health issues and medical conditions whose very procedures and treatments ravaged their young bodies.

I decided that I was going to find a way to offer a "positive spin" on all of the health issue negatives and to create a portal of communication and a treasure of heartwarming and reassuring perspectives to those "hands off" subjects.

Additionally I want to inspire a muffled laugh, instigate a tiny smile, mischievous giggle or just create an environmental change and safe place for even a brief moment that would add a sparkle to a weary eye.

AND I was going to give a comforting and supportive symbolic "hug" to each patient and reader by filling them with a sense of pride in themselves for having endured their own health battle and surrounding issues. Plus, I would provide a tangible and permanent way to honor and celebrate their courage!

I was unable to have children, so this is my way of giving back. In 1987 the Just Plain Love® Charitable Trust was born."

Brent Atwater's Other Dream: Just® Plays, Performances & Educational Programs for Children with "Poof" the Angel & "Friend" the pet angel therapy dog. Surely, Ms. Atwater dreams, there can be participatory mini skits/plays held in healthcare and medical facilities lasting about 5 to 15 minutes that would hold a patient's attention, entertain, educate, rehabilitate and provide a few safe moments of mental relief through laughter, plus providing each patient with a tangible Badge of Honor to reward and recognize their courage.

For the past 20+ years Brent Atwater has researched, tested, rewritten and reworked each children's healing book and play according to the storytelling responses and reactions from healthy and unhealthy readers, caregivers, family, friends, medical and healthcare professionals, clients and her storytelling audience.

Brent Atwater's hope is to inspire the creative imagination of readers of all ages to replace negative thoughts about health issues, medical experiences, rehabilitative therapy and reentry into society with a positive "spin" on their journey to health and well-being.

Visit
www.BrentAtwater.com
www.JustPlainLoveBooks.com

Just Plain Love® Books
inspiring thoughts that provide smiles, hugs and healing for every reader's heart!

Other Just Plain Love® Titles
are translated into other languages and
Available in Audio, EBooks, Hardcover, Kindle and Paperback

Inspirational:
The Beach Book: Beach Lessons for a Workaholic!

Children's Books:
Cancer Kids—God's Special Children!
Cancer and MY Daddy

Life and Spiritual Purpose:
How to Accept, Trust & Live Your Life's Spiritual
Purpose: Am I Worthy?
Prayers to Empower Your Life's Spiritual Purpose

Energy Medicine, Intuitive Development:
Medical Intuition, Intuitive Diagnosis, MIDI- How to
See Inside a Body
AMIDI - Animal Medical Intuitive Diagnostic
Imaging™

Self Help and Healing, Mind Body Medicine:
Healing Yourself! 23 Ways to Heal YOU!
Paintings that Heal! Art is the Medicine

Animal Lovers' Books:
the Dog with a "B" on His Bottom!
"I'm Home!" a Dog's Never Ending Love Story
"I'm Home!" a Cat's Never Ending Love Story
"I'm Home!" a Horse's Never Ending Love Story
Animal Life after Death & Pet Reincarnation
Answers for all your heart's Questions!
La Réincarnation des Animaux de Compagnie
動物は生まれ変わる

We hope you enjoyed our
Just Plain Love® Book.

Visit Brent Atwater's websites:
www.BrentAtwater.com
www.JustPlainLoveBooks.com
www.BrentEnergyWork.com

elieve
In
Reincarnation
It's Real!

Friend is available
for paw signings,
guest appearances,
fundraising & hugs!

As are some of the
other wonderful
reincarnated pets that
have shared their
stories

Join Brent & Friend's
Global Community
of Groups & Pages on:
Facebook, Twitter,
YouTube, LinkedIn,
MySpace and more!

Printed in Great Britain
by Amazon.co.uk, Ltd.,
Marston Gate.